THE SCREWLOOSE LECTURES

Larry
Richards

THE SCREWLOOSE LECTURES

Studies in
the Ethics of Hell

WORD BOOKS
PUBLISHER
WACO, TEXAS

Preface and Disclaimer

My name appears on the title page of this book, but I would like to renounce, here and now, any claim to its authorship. The *real* author of this book is a certain Screwloose, who is a—well—demon in the Kingdom of Hell. It seems this demon delivered a series of lectures at something called "Underworld University," a training school for Tempters and Deceivers.

As far as I can surmise, this Screwloose, who is an experienced field agent and a supervisor of fiends assigned to deceive various individual humans, was ordered by Hell Central to give a series of lectures on ethics. (He defines ethics, by the way, as "getting humans to do the right thing from the wrong motive or the wrong thing from the right motive and thus enabling them to sin comfortably.") The lectures were taped, and transcripts were apparently sent to a demon with whom Screwloose was feuding—one Glubnose, Dean of Faculty at Underworld University.

Which is where I come in. While attacking the cacti in the backyard of my Phoenix, Arizona home, I recently came across the transcripts and some correspondence, crammed into a ragged manila envelope and lying among pieces of a broken pottery jar. As to how it came to be there, I hesitate to speculate. It has been suggested to me that perhaps Glubnose placed them there, hoping to get Screwloose in trouble with Hell Central for a breach of security. But I doubt this theory very much; it seems more likely to me that the manuscript appeared by accident, the result of a sloppy mail system or some other form of infernal carelessness.

Any other speculations about the Screwloose lectures I leave in the hands of the reader. I merely present them as I found them, with the hope that they may prove instructive.

LARRY RICHARDS
Phoenix, Arizona

 UNDERWORLD UNIVERSITY

September 12, 32912

Screwloose
Field Supervisor
Department of Temptry
Level 13

My Dear Screwloose:

I have been directed by Lower Authority to invite
you to accept the post of Visiting Lecturer in
ethics for the spring quarter, 32913.

Clearance has been granted by the Department of
Temptry for your leave of absence to accept this
ministry.

Please confirm immediately.

Glubnose

Glubnose
Dean of Faculty
Underworld University
Level 6

---

*Note: Screwloose and Glubnose use a dating based on the fall of man in Eden.
They most carefully avoid any references to the human dating system, which is
based on the incarnation of the Enemy. The corresponding human date to 32912 is
believed to be A.D. 1979.

Department of Temptry

September 24, 32912

Glubnose
Dean of Faculty
Underworld University
Level 6

Dear Glubnose:

That invitation of yours is quite an honor. But
I am sure you're aware of my attitude toward all
such "classroom" attempts to train demons. All my
experience tells me that it is here, on the front
lines, guiding fiends engaged in battle with the
Enemy, that tempters are made. It would be a waste
of my time--particularly now as the climax of our
ages-long warfare draws near--to desert my post for
the isolation of the ivory pit.

An ivory pit that you, my dear Glubnose, have remained in far too long!

So accept my regrets. I am not suited by tempera-
ment, inclination, or experience for academic duty.

Sincerely,

Screwloose

Screwloose

 UNDERWORLD UNIVERSITY

October 1, 32912

Screwloose
Field Supervisor
Department of Temptry
Level 13

Screwloose:

I have been instructed by Lower Authority to correct
my earlier letter. You are not _invited_ to accept
the post of Visiting Lecturer in ethics this coming
spring. You are _directed_ to accept the post.

The Department of Temptry has been informed of this
decision, and of the fact that Professor Slobglub
has been chosen to assume your duties while you are
absent.

This decision follows a new policy, formulated by
our Academic Excellence Committee, and designed to
"give academicians practical experience while expos-
ing students to fiends with actual field experience."

Please confirm immediately.

Glubnose

Glubnose
Dean of Faculty
Underworld University
Level 6

P.S. Personally I am convinced that this is a dam-
nable policy, one which will ultimately destroy the
integrity of our academic degree. The thought of
having to bear with _you_ in this program fills me
with disgust and shame.

Department of Temptry

October 21, 32912

Glubnose
Dean of Faculty
Underworld University
Level 6

My very dear Glubnose,

Your last letter encourages me! I take great comfort in knowing that you are against this new program. Based on my assessment of your insight (an
assessment which has not changed across the millenniums since, as young and idealistic demons, we
chose to flee the Enemy with Our Father Below), I
am convinced that there will be great value in the
new program.

In fact, I am already toying with a new structure
for the ethics course which I found so completely
boring under old Slobglub. Should you choose to
sit in on a class or two, you'll never recognize
it!!

With growing enthusiasm,

Screwloose
Screwloose

 UNDERWORLD UNIVERSITY

October 29, 32912

Screwloose
Field Supervisor
Department of Temptry
Level 13

Screwloose:

I order you, as Dean of Faculty, not to deviate from
the traditional syllabus of the ethics course. Simply use the notes you took as a student under Slobglub, and try to state his thoughts with some semblance
of his dignity and intellectual capacity.

Unfortunately, I will not be able to sit in on any
of your classes. I have been assigned (as part of
the same sick and "innovative" program that forces
you on dear old UU) to spend the quarter as an observer on Level 14. But I assure you that I will
receive reports on your teaching. And should you
in any way disregard my orders, I will do everything inhumanly possible to see you singed!

Glubnose

Glubnose
Dean of Faculty
Underworld University
Level 6

Department of Temptry

November 3, 32912

Glubnose
Dean of Faculty
Underworld University
Level 6

Dear old Glubnose,

Congratulations on your promotion! At last you are
going to get out into the real world, where you might
actually learn something.

As for your spies, don't give it a second thought.
I intend to make transcriptions of all my lectures,
and will send you manuscripts weekly.

I am sure you will enjoy them. The thought of you,
captive on Level 14 and unable to do anything but
squirm, will give me unutterable enjoyment, and no
doubt will spur me on to unusual creativity.

As for old Slobglub's notes, I burned those as soon
as I passed the final exam. My only real regret
now is that he may influence some of my junior tempters when he replaces me for the semester. However,
I have warned them all to ignore him.

Cordially,

Screwloose

Professor Screwloose

 UNDERWORLD UNIVERSITY

January 14, 32913

Glubnose
Observer, 3rd Class
Level 14

Dear Glubnose,

I have taken up residence in your old cubbyhole here
at UU, and I find it very cozy indeed. Nor have
I forgotten my promise to forward you transcripts
of my classes (the first lecture is enclosed).

It's good to see so many alert young devils in my
course. I actually believe I'm going to enjoy teaching them--especially if in the process I can make them
completely dissatisfied with the way "education" is
generally dispensed down here.

Of course, there wasn't too much I could do in the
first lecture. Tradition says there are things one
must cover in first lectures, no matter what. But
as we move on in the course, I hope to liven it up
a bit. As for the stuffy tomes we used in studying
ethics--they'll not be cracked in this course.

I see, by the way, no need for further correspondence.
If you have comments, you may send them on. But I
doubt that I'll have time to read them.

Warmly,

Screwloose

Screwloose

LECTURE ONE
Tuesday, 15 January 32913

Introduction: The Ethics of Hell

My name is Screwloose. I am your instructor this semester in ethics. But let me warn you. I am *not* a teacher. I am not a philosopher. I am simply a practical, hard-working fiend who has spent centuries on the battlefield, and many more centuries as a field supervisor in the Department of Temptry. I have not read an ethics book (either human or demon) in millenniums, and I certainly do not intend to read one now. What I intend to do is to discuss practical ethics—to explore with you the simple, daily situations in which human beings are called on to make ethical choices. My goal is to demonstrate how the ethics of Hell can be best applied to help move humans on their downward path.

Now about ethics. Ethics can be defined simply as the art of encouraging human beings to do the right thing from the wrong motives, or the wrong thing from the right motives. You'll note that this definition rules out the classical goal of demonic ethics developed by that old fool Slobglub—to encourage humans to do the wrong thing from the wrong motives. In practice this is to be avoided. Such acts are so clearly *un*ethical that even humans will be hard put to rationalize them away, and one day may be convicted of sin. However, if we can encourage actions which are at least *partly* good, we can easily focus a client's attention on that "good" element and lead him to be highly insulted should anyone, even his own conscience, suggest that somehow his actions carry the taint of sin.

Of course, there is no need to point out that we never want humans to do the right thing from the right motives. Admittedly, they will never do *anything* very well. But when they begin, even feebly, to attempt righteousness motivated by love, the Enemy takes delight in them.

Let's remember, then, that the ethics of Hell is based on

helping human beings be *partly* good—never wholly good, and never wholly evil. There's nothing like a mixed good to, as one of my clients used to say, "grease the skids," and help a human being slide complacently into Hell.

I must at this point note that there is an ethics of Heaven as well as an ethics of Hell. It's a contemptible ethics, one that overlooks the nature of those weak and watery creatures the Enemy claims to love. It disregards their muddled thinking, the cloudy currents of emotion that sweep them, and the uncertain will that hesitates over even the clearest of choices. It overlooks the fact that they are lower beings, created (as the Enemy's handbook admits) "lower than the angels," and it seeks to form a reflection of the Enemy Himself in their personalities.

This is hard for us to grasp. These contemptible, short-lived cattle, fit only to be sucked dry and the juices of their misery enjoyed by us, actually do bear stamped in their personalities some echo of the Eternal. Even those who have not yet voluntarily joined the Enemy have some remnant of His image. That remnant He may at any time choose to activate. Then, despite our most desperate efforts, we sometimes see the work of decades melt before our eyes. When that melting comes, and their personalities yield to Him, then they *do* reflect His likeness. Then the dust of death reminds us that their destiny is to be raised above us, to sit with Him and bear His image as perfectly as He Himself once stooped to take up theirs.

When that happens, we know the meaning of hate. And they know the meaning of love.

But please. Don't let me discourage you. In fact, the advantage is mostly ours. There's little you can suggest to them that they won't already be inclined to do. That first foolish pair joined our Father below willingly, and all the rest reflect *that* far more than they mirror the Enemy. So we have the advantage as we help them remain fit to spend Eternity in our presence.

Now, the course. I believe that to understand and to apply the ethics of Hell we need to explore three areas. These are reflected in the three units into which this course has been divided. First, we need to look at the psychology of ethics, and understand what aspects of the human personality we can use in our campaign. Second, we need to look at the language of ethics; the more we can cloud the human mind to the real import of ethical terms and concepts, the easier it will be for us to help them sin complacently. (Remember, the comfortable sin is always to be preferred to the one that pricks the conscience, even though the vibrations of more intense evil might give us greater temporary pleasure.) And finally, we want to explore some of the opportunities the contemporary world gives us to confuse their ethical thinking, and to engage even strong believers in crusades which, in one way or other, detour them into sin.

One of the most promising, by the way, is known in the United States as "women's liberation." This subject is puzzling to us whose personalities are uncomplicated by sex. But it can prove very enjoyable, for it can provide us with many opportunities for twisting human lives out of the Enemy's pattern.

Now, one last word before we cut this first class short and retire to the Student Union for some liquid refreshment. Many of you have hesitated to take this course. I notice that a number of you are upperclassmen. You've put off taking ethics, even though it's recommended for freshmen and sophomores.

Let me reassure you. Ethics is not a difficult subject. It's a delightful one. During this course you will discover hundreds of ways to spoil the lives of your human clients—a prospect any blood-lusting demon finds delightful. Most important, you will multiply your pleasure on the battlefield. Master ethics, and you will know the exaltation that comes to us when a human life that the Enemy seeks to enrich becomes sour and spoiled.

Ultimately this is what the ethics of Hell is about. It is about *our* pleasure. It is about the human agony and suffering on which we feed. It is about denying *them* the slightest taste of joy.

And now, my fiends, our first class is over. Pick up your syllabus on the way out. And be ready for a fiendishly delightful course!

Ethics of Hell
Professor Screwloose
Spring Quarter, 32913

Syllabus

1. Introduction: The Ethics of Hell

   I. The Psychology of Ethics: The Human
      Personality

2. Perception: Through a Glass, Darkly
3. Emotion: The Troubled Sea
4. Motivation: The Perilous Passions
5. Belief: The Comfortable Illusion
6. Will: Practical Paralysis

   II. The Language of Ethics: The Power of Words

7. Law: The Stone God
8. Freedom: The Fleeting Fantasy
9. Authority: The Chains of Command
10. Truth: The Outer Limit
11. Guilt: The Lost Connection
12. Forgiveness: The Extinction of Pride
13. Love: A Maze of Love
14. Love: The Enemy's Way

   III. The Opportunities of Ethics: Contemporary
      Issues

15. Capital Punishment: Societal Imperatives
16. Homosexuality: Private Depravity
17. Women's Liberation: Cultural Distortions
18. Abortion: A Private Doctrine

PART I

The Psychology of Ethics:
The Human Personality

LECTURE TWO
Thursday, 17 January 32913

Perception: Through a Glass, Darkly

One of the most pleasant pastimes for a demon on duty is reading over a client's shoulder. No, I don't mean watching the motions of sin set to swaying by his reading "adult" literature. Oh no. I mean listening through his thoughts to some of the foolishness that wise men have put in print.

I remember my discovery of the fact that human beings actually view ethics as a branch of philosophy. Philosophy, as you know, has been defined by humans as "the rational investigation of the truths and principles of being, knowledge, or conduct."* The assumption that human beings might penetrate to the first principles of anything using their rational faculties is beyond belief to us who see the dullness of their mental processes. But it's even more absurd to imagine them approaching the subject of ethics rationally.

The fact is, human beings act irrationally. Of course, later on they do invent reasons for what they've done. But the roots of their choices are very seldom located in their intellects. Thus the philosopher's notion that if a man knows the good he will do it is ridiculous beyond words. (Humans trace this notion back to Plato, but we more accurately trace it to some early creative work by our Department of Dissimulation.)

You'll notice, by the way, so much evidence that doing good does *not* follow knowing good that you will be constantly amazed that humans themselves accept such foolishness. You'll see fat men, whose laboring hearts pound and whose breath comes short at a flight of stairs, who *know* they need to diet, choose the richest pastry and comfort themselves with the thought that "tomorrow" they'll begin. You'll see men and women whose relatives have died of lung cancer pick up packs of cigarettes on which are

Random House Dictionary of the English Language.

printed, "The Surgeon General has determined that cigarette smoking is dangerous to your health." You'll see government agencies spend millions of tax dollars to publicize the dangers of smoking, while other government agencies spend millions of tax dollars to subsidize the farmers who grow tobacco. You'll see Christians who are sure they should spend more time muddling through the Enemy's handbook settle down instead to watch some inane television show whose plot they've seen a hundred times before.

And these same people, in club or classroom, will mumble wisely about ethics, and persist in imagining that if only one knows the good he will do it. And they will be satisfied that the task of ethics is to help men *know*.

Now, this suits our purpose perfectly. We hope that humans never realize that ethics is not a rational discipline at all. But, my young fiends, it does not suit the purpose of Our Father Below if you and I are confused at this point. So encourage humans to explore ethics books and argue wisely about hierarchies of good. Humans who spend enough time studying ethics seldom stumble onto the reality of spontaneously living out the ethics of Heaven. It is against this, the spontaneous living of a life that is ethical by Enemy standards, that all our efforts must be marshaled. Spontaneously doing the Enemy's will is at the heart of Enemy ethics and this, believe me, is hardly ever grounded in that calm and rational approach to analyzing principles and truths that humans value and call "philosophy."

So practical ethics demands that we take a very different approach. We reject the approach of the philosopher, and begin instead with the psychology of human beings. We want to catch a glimpse of a whole bundle of psychological factors that clog, confuse, and yet move men to make ethical decisions. The first of these psychological factors is listed in your syllabus as "perception."

This is, as I have said, a practical course. Those of you who expected some abstract lecture about perception in the philosophic sense will be disappointed. But I will always ask the practical question. Today that question is this: What perception by a human has the greatest impact on his ethical behavior?

The answer is that human choices are most often shaped by an individual's perception of *himself*.

Human beings have their origins in time. You must remember

this. They lack the clear perspective of directly created beings. We demons know who we are. We remember our bursting forth full grown at the Enemy's word. We remember that great leap upward to self-determination we made with Lucifer, that moment the Enemy perversely calls a "fall." We even know the future of our race. Oh yes. We know, and have the courage to face ourselves. But none of this is true of humans. Their self-awareness grows bit by tiny bit. Even their greatest saints hardly know who they really are. At best they only grasp dimly the unfolding germ of Enemy life He planted at the moment of faith.

It's because humans cannot see themselves that they so often stumble. They're tripped up by unreal images that masquerade as reality. Properly manipulated, a client's distorted self-perceptions can be used by us to keep him from ever breaking out into the freedom of the "sons of God," as the followers of the enemy are disgustingly called.

A human begins to acquire a perception of himself in childhood. Mother may tie his shoes till he's nearly six . . . and he accepts her evaluation of him as her "little boy." Later Dad shouts in anger when he takes a third strike in his first ball game. Children who grow up in homes like this begin to see themselves as their parents see them. They develop a perception of themselves as weak, inadequate, and unlovely. Through it all, the child feels the pain of rejection, and learns to fear the loss of his parents' love. This typically marks him with a lifelong unwillingness to risk.

By the way. Those of you assigned to parents must see that they develop quite unrealistic expectations for their boys and girls. Whisper to a parent that a child of six months must be spanked if he or she cries at night, so that the child will "learn to obey." Tell fathers to beat their sons when they do something wrong, in order to "break their sinful will." And do twit frantic mothers with the fear that unless their teens read the Bible daily they will surely lose their faith in college. All such expectations will be expressed, with appropriate signs of disappointment, in little ways that crush a child's spirit. And in each case we will be well on our way to shaping another human whose distorted view of himself will keep him in our camp.

You see, humans who perceive themselves as weak invariably draw back from decisions. Such people desperately *want* to make right choices, but are so convinced of their inadequacy and so afraid of failure that they're unable to act.

This, of course, is one of those mixed goods that we seek to stimulate. Let a person take comfort in his *intentions*. He'll console himself with the thought, "God knows I *want* to serve Him," and thus excuse the fact that he never actually chooses to serve. You want to actively encourage the desire of a person like this to serve God. Fill his thoughts with visions of what he hopes to do for God. Encourage him to pray fervently for strength. Let him feel proud of the purity of his motives. But when the time comes to act, remind him of his weakness, and tell him he must wait for God to give him strength before he takes a single step. His perception of himself as weak will dominate; he will *want* but never *do* the Enemy's will.

On the other hand, some humans have early experiences which lead them to see themselves as strong. Their parents love them unconditionally, give them regular responsibilities, and help them successfully accomplish each set task. In school they have athletic or social or academic success. Their perception of themselves usually makes them willing to act where those who see themselves as weak hold back.

Actually, the human who sees himself as strong is just as vulnerable as the weak. Even the strongest human isn't strong enough. The Enemy is as concerned about an inner attitude of love and dependence on Him as He is with outward behavior. The strong will act . . . but may act in such self-reliance that the inner man can be molded by us.

I recommend you lead the strong to philosophies like those of Emmanuel Kant, which prate about "ought implying can." A strong person will be attracted to this kind of thinking. He will feel that because he ought to live the Enemy's way he somehow can, and will rush out to face life in his own strength. He may never realize that without Enemy intervention the best he can do will twist itself into sin.

It's helpful for you to persuade the strong to fix on one particular moral injunction—and then ensure them success with it. I once had a client who determined early in life to remain unmarried until he reached the age of the Enemy at crucifixion. He struggled with normal passions, and I helped him overcome them. He reached age thirty a virgin, and was easily persuaded to continue his chaste course.

All the time I was working to twist his achievement into pride. It was a short step then to develop contempt for "weaker" men and women whose "baser passions" forced them to marry. Before long he developed strong notions about the "wantonness" of perfectly innocent behavior he noticed in younger Christian girls. Within a few years, his moral "success" had fathered a host of sins that cut him off from other Christians and replaced love for the brotherhood with an attitude of judgment and condemnation.

I hope you see my point. The perception that a human has of himself will dramatically influence his approach to life. If he has what human psychologists call a "poor self-image," he will usually *want* to do what he believes to be the right thing, but he will not *try to do it,* because he is convinced he can't.

If he has what human psychologists call a "good self-image," he is likely to attempt what he feels to be his duty. But his failure to depend on the Enemy may lead his sinful nature to express itself in all sorts of side effects, such as pride, lack of compassion for "weaker" humans, and so on.

Either of these self-perceptions is perfectly adaptable to our purposes. A sensible demon will base his manipulations of a client on that particular human's image of himself.

Now a word of warning. Each of the self-perceptions I have described is in fact illusory. Each describes what a client *thinks himself to be*—not what he really is. The Enemy's strategy is to help a human discover himself as the Enemy perceives him, not as he sees himself.

The Enemy's perception of these loathsome beasts is so disgustingly different from our own that I can hardly bring myself to describe it. But you must understand it if you are to be alert to danger signs in a client's consciousness.

The Enemy actually appreciates humans as ethically *unable,* but *enableable.* His handbook describes them brutally; it condemns them as unrighteous, calls their throats open graves, their lips poisonous, their mouths full of cursing and bitterness, their feet swift to shed blood. This catalog of what we see as positive virtues is no praise from Him. It is instead the sternest condemnation of human character and behavior. Yet the Enemy goes on to insist that, even though He can expect nothing of humans, He loves and values them! In an act of what He calls "grace," He Himself crawled into history and in a most contemptible way bowed His shoulders to receive the blow His own justice decreed.

He has the gall to invite humans to accept themselves, both the strong and the weak, as He accepts them. As having failed, yet still of infinite value to Him. As beings whom He plans not to *use,* as we would, but to bestow with lavish, undeserved gifts and raise to Himself.

So when the peculiar transaction the Enemy calls "faith" has led humans to respond, He wants their attention to shift completely from themselves to Him. The weak are to realize that His strength is perfected in weakness. The strong are to rejoice that, as He says, "apart from Me you can do nothing." * When their vision is cleared, and their sense of self no longer a hindrance, the Enemy promises that He will do in them what they cannot do themselves. Then, by His despicable presence in their lives, the Enemy twists the glorious complexities of sin that we find so rich and refreshing into dull and heavy strands of righteousness.

But, thank Hell, this is difficult for even Him to do. Humans must, in His words, deny themselves to become themselves. They must lose their old lives to find the new. As long as humans persist in viewing life through the lenses of their own self-perceptions, we will realize the benefits of what that old complainer Paul writes of as seeing "through a glass, darkly." The dim and distorted view they have of reality will come clear for them the day they meet the Enemy face to face. But, until then, any one of them who sees himself as either strong or weak is sure to be our prey.

Class dismissed.

---

*Note: Scripture references in Screwloose's lectures are often paraphrased in his own words, and seem to be renderings from the original Greek or Hebrew. Screwloose does not give references: possibly he is quoting from early manuscripts not yet divided into chapters and verses. However, an appendix lists the references found by the editor's research.

Department of Temptry

January 18, 32913

Screwloose
Underworld University
Level 6

For Hell's sake, what _are_ you thinking of?

I've never heard such heresy in all my aeons in Our
Father's dark domain. It's bad enough to ridicule
your betters, who for millenniums have taught ethics
from a firm philosophical base. But to actually encourage humans to "pray fervently" . . . to actually
encourage them to want to serve God, or to act on
what they feel they ought to do . . . why, you'll
produce a class of demons that plays right into the
Enemy's hands.

Dear damnation! Screwloose, I have heard human preachers exhort their congregations to exactly the same
things you suggest we demons should encourage in our
clients. Whose side are you on anyway?

I tell you plainly that you are to return at once to
the traditional approach to teaching ethics. What's
more, a copy of your lecture has been sent Special
Delivery to Lower Authority. If you won't listen to
me, you will most certainly listen to them, and fear
the terrors they can release on any of us at will.

Furiously,

Glubnose

Glubnose
Dean of Faculty (on leave)

LECTURE THREE
Tuesday, 22 January 32913

Emotion: The Troubled Sea

One of my many pleasant experiences in the field illustrates the ethical potential of human emotions. It happened during a meeting of a small group of the Enemy's followers. This group had been coming together regularly to study the Enemy's handbook, to make rather insipid prayers, and to "share." Unfortunately, they were drawing closer to each other and to the Enemy. It was time for definite action on our part.

The leader of the group, a human male called Vince, was my client at the time. I called a meeting of the agents assigned to others in the group, and together we worked out a strategy.

On the target evening all went as usual until just before closing time. Then Bloblub's client, a female named Jan, exploded. Jan was an unstable human, whom Bloblub had guided into a "therapy group" where the leader encouraged everyone to "express their feelings." This was of course something we wanted to encourage.

Bloblub had worked all that day to build Jan's feelings of anger and frustration. He had twitched her irritation at the red light she had to stop for on the way to the store. When the car stalled, he had reminded her that her husband had *promised* to have it tuned. Anger at a broken fingernail that snagged her pantyhose had been amplified; it had become just one more piece of evidence that no one, not even the Enemy, cared about all Jan had to suffer! All these little pressures we had helped build up during the day. That night, Vince made some comment that triggered the reaction we had planned.

Jan blew up at Vince. He made her so mad! He was domineering and insensitive. She was tired of his controlling the group, forcing his thinking on them. Jan made it very plain that

Vince had no right to think of himself as a spiritual leader. He wasn't a servant; he was a dictator!

Jan also took shots at a few others, including one young woman very new to the Enemy's camp. Everyone was so stunned that there was no answer; the group broke up shortly.

That night each of us had a lovely time with our clients. Vince went home and actually cried. He was particularly vulnerable just then; many business problems had drained him emotionally. Carol, the young believer Jan had attacked, was deeply hurt too. And the others—why, the more they thought about what Jan had done, the more angry they became.

The next day Carol phoned Vince's wife, and—though I struggled to prevent it—Vince and his wife went to talk with Jan. Vince apologized for anything he might have done that was domineering or controlling and asked forgiveness. Fortunately, Bloblub was able to whisper in Jan's ear that this apology simply confirmed her opinion, so she accepted the apology self-righteously.

Vince and his wife told Jan how hurt Carol was, and suggested she call Carol and apologize. Later that day Jan did call Carol, and sweetly suggested that Carol see a counselor in the church who would "help you get over your feelings of persecution." Later, Jan told Vince's wife that she'd learned an important lesson; she would never again keep her feelings bottled up so long that when they came out people would misunderstand. She'd say what she felt right away, as soon as she felt it!

Now, young fiends, divide up into groups of four and talk about this incident. What does it tell you about a human's ethical vulnerability? What misunderstandings of emotion and feeling did Bloblub and I and the others use to bring about what happened? Let's see what you can come up with, and then I'll return to share with you my own analysis.

* * *

Quiet. Quiet please.

I've been listening to your discussions, fellow demons. I must say you are either not yet capable of clear thinking, or you have received totally inadequate training here at UU.

Singlaub. You seemed pleased with those feelings of hurt and anger Jan provoked. The feelings were, I admist, tasty—a tiny nibble of the fruit of human anguish you and I feed on. But no matter how tasty such feelings are, they are ethically neutral until expressed in some action.

Think, Singlaub. The human male, Vince, was hurt enough to cry. But in spite of his hurt (and there was anger there, too), the next day Vince actually went to Jan, and *he* apologized! Those feelings of hurt and anger, which might have led to a lovely feud, or to delicious backbiting, or at least to a frigid barrier between Vince and Jan, instead led to apology! Vince actually chose to follow a path specifically laid down by the Enemy for His people to follow when hurts and sins interrupt their fellowship! What humans would call negative feelings led to what the Enemy would call a positive ethical action. Can't you see that it's not how a person feels but what he *does* that is ethical or unethical?

Now Jan, on the other hand, had some of the same feelings that she provoked in the others. She was angry and upset about all the things that had happened to her that day. In the group she released those feelings and expressed them in what the Enemy calls "acts of the sinful nature." She spoke out in hatred, sowed discord, and had an absolutely delightful fit of rage. As long as her feelings remained hers, inside her, they too had no positive or negative ethical value. But as soon as she chose to act in harmony with those feelings, *then* ethics became involved.

This, Singlaub—and you others—is the first thing you must learn about human emotions. They can and are to be bent by us to stimulate actions that accord with the ethics of Hell. But feelings themselves, as that disgusting reformer Luther once said about temptations, are like birds flitting around one's head. No human can keep them from flying there. But one can keep them from building a nest in his hair.

What can we do, then, to make sure that human emotions do lead to truly ethical behavior? How can we be sure that as many emotions as possible will stimulate sin? The answer to that one is, let's keep humans as confused as possible in their thinking about feelings. Particularly, you want to encourage these notions:

1. *Feelings are the ultimate reality.* Every human knows that his feelings are real. Feelings are *there;* they are experienced. A wise demon can use the subjective reality of feelings to convince a client that his feelings are the *ultimate* reality.

A wife may feel neglected by a busy husband. She feels ignored and unimportant. When she's feeling sorry for herself, it's easy to convince her that her husband actually does not care about her.

His actual attitude toward her is no longer important. Her feelings are all that count, and she'll begin to think and act on the basis of what she feels, rather than what her husband actually thinks or wants or feels.

A follower of the Enemy will usually feel frightened if he has a chance to speak up about his faith. The fear, the feelings of inadequacy, are so vivid that you can easily convince him the feelings match reality. You can suggest there *is* something to fear, and that he really *is* hopelessly inadequate. Why, if he speaks up, he'll be sure to say something wrong, and will probably drive the other person away from the Enemy instead of helping him come near!

In cases like these, you want to focus the attention of your clients on their feelings. Amplify the feelings. Let the client be totally caught up in them. Never, never let the client question his feelings. If that wife ever questioned her feelings, she might ask her husband what *he* actually feels about her!

"Do you still love me?" she might blurt out one evening.

"Why, of course I do," he would say in reply.

"But . . ." and now the sniffles would begin . . . "you, well, you don't *talk* to me anymore. I feel sort of deserted, like I'm not important to you."

"Oh, honey. I'm sorry. It's just that, well, we've got a new management team at the plant. To tell you the truth, I'm not sure they'll keep me on. I haven't wanted to worry you, with the kids just ready to start high school and all. But, well, it has been bothering me. I guess I just didn't realize how it affected me at home."

Now, what a disgusting turn of events *that* would be. All that beautiful alienation spoiled just because that foolish woman questions her feelings enough to ask her husband if he *really* doesn't care any more. When she shares her feelings, he is able to explain his actions, and suddenly she grasps the true situation. You can imagine what happens to all those potentially useful feelings of hurt and humiliation. Yes. They're replaced by totally unsuitable feelings such as sympathy and concern for *him!*

Or suppose that fearful little coward's attention wanders from his feelings of fright and inadequacy. He might remember the promise of the Enemy, "I am with you always." Now, that's a reality *we* fear. If the Enemy's follower sees that reality, he's likely to act and to speak out *in spite* of his feelings! I've seen that all too often. When the cattle do act in obedience, even such a delightful emotion as abject fear changes to a sense of inner joy.

Now then, you and I understand that, although a human's feelings have subjective reality, they do not have ultimate reality. We know how fickle human emotions are, how easily feelings change. But never let a human think even for a moment that in a given situation there are factors to be considered other than his feelings. Keep the focus on feelings; your clients will quite naturally accept their emotions as reality.

2. *Feelings must be expressed.* Much of modern humanistic therapy is based on twin notions about the reality of feelings and the need for them to be "expressed." Some therapists believe that acting out negative feelings—shouting in anger, verbally abusing an irritating person, or kicking a chair—*ventilates* the feelings. The theory is, if you *let* them out, you *get* them out.

This is very helpful from our point of view. "Expressing" anger by attacking another person or even an inanimate object brings emotion into the realm of action. (You remember, it is when feelings find expression in action that they become ethical issues.) Also, as even human research has shown, acting out negative feelings does not reduce them; it actually makes the feelings more intense. The more a person shouts out his anger at others, the more likely he is to be angry. So the idea that feelings must be let out is a notion we certainly want to cultivate.

To cultivate such a notion within the Enemy camp, your strategy should be to link acting out feelings with "honesty." This of course is how Jan justified her tirade against Vince and Carol. She really did feel angry at them. How could she be honest, and not tell them how she felt?

Of course, Jan never really did express her feelings. Jan didn't say, "I feel pushed around," or "I feel rejected because no one cares about my opinions." Not at all. What she actually did was to accuse Vince of dominating and dictating to the group.

This is a very helpful confusion to encourage. It's obvious that anyone who really is expressing his or her feelings will have to talk about "I"—"I feel pushed around," or, "I feel rejected."

Those kinds of statements express feelings, because they tell what is happening inside. But this is something that, no matter how obvious, humans seldom see. Instead, they make all sorts of statements about "you"—"You are domineering," "You are insensitive." And then they justify these verbal attacks by saying, "I was simply expressing my feelings"—when the feelings were never expressed at all!

It is, by the way, quite helpful for humans to *actually* express their feelings. The Enemy's handbook, and especially the Book of Psalms, shows how freely these cattle can tell their feelings to the Enemy. In nearly every case, a psalm which begins with frustration or anger or envy, or some other emotion helpful to us, shows that, as the feeling is shared, the Enemy works within the human to change the feeling to peace or joy.

When humans really share their feelings with each other, all sorts of dismaying things can happen. Like the neglected wife, they may discover that the feelings do not fit reality. And when reality is faced, human feelings do change. When a person like Jan, whose whole approach to life tended to be unstable and unhappy, shares her feelings instead of hurling them like spears at others, she finds that others support her and care. That flood of care and support can also cause feelings to change.

So, fiends, again. Keep your client's attention on his or her feelings. Never let him ask whether his feelings fit reality; let him assume that, because the feelings are subjectively real, they represent a true appraisal of his situation. Never, never let a client tell others his feelings in that revealing "I feel" way. Keep him thinking that "expressing feelings" means attacking others or shouting out his anger or frustration. It won't be hard to do these things. Humans would much rather believe our illusions than deal with the Enemy's truth.

3. *Feelings are caused by others.* This is another confusion we want to encourage. Again, it's an easy confusion to maintain. Humans have built it into their language and thinking.

"You make me so happy."

"You make me sad."

"You make me angry."

You'll often hear phrases like this in their conversation. What they are doing is *making others responsible for their emotional reactions.*

Now, you yourself may be confused at this point. It is true that as a field agent you will, as Bloblub did with Jan, attempt to "make a client angry." Bloblub amplified Jan's irritation at the red light. He reminded her that her husband had promised to have the car engine tuned. He intensified the anger she felt when she snagged her pantyhose. His goal was to build up frustration so she would explode at the group meeting—and Bloblub succeeded.

But it's important for you to realize that even the most efficient demon can never *make* a human angry or frustrated by such strategies. Jan might have shrugged off the long red light. She might have been amused at her husband's forgetfulness; after all, many wives have learned to be amused at their husbands' weaknesses. She might simply have said, "Oops. I knew I should have fixed that nail," and gotten another pair of hose from the dresser. But she didn't. Jan reacted to each of these annoyances with growing anger. Jan's *reaction* to the incidents was the true source of her feelings.

Consider another example: a human being might be driving along the road and be unexpectedly passed by a driver going well over the speed limit. Some humans who find themselves in such a situation would react by honking their horns angrily. Others might try to catch and outrace the speeder. Some would simply curse the gas hog. A few might wonder what the emergency is, and even offer a prayer that the Enemy would meet the unknown need.

Now, does the speeding driver *make* the one person honk the horn angrily? Or does he *make* another curse? Or *make* another challenge to a race? Or, Hell forbid, does the speeder *make* one pray? Of course not. The response each person makes is his or her own choice. Each one is responsible for the anger or the concern that he or she feels.

What I am saying here is that a human being "owns" his own emotions. They are not forced on him or her by any other individual or by any outward circumstance.

This is of course another fact that you should never let humans grasp. If a human ever accepts responsibility for his own emotional reactions, you are in a bad way indeed. The human may turn to the Enemy and share his feelings in prayer, or ask Him for help in responding differently. He may even share his feelings with other humans, in order to test his emotions against reality.

The reason this is dangerous to us is that the Enemy works in a human being's emotional nature as well as in other dimensions of his personality. When He talks about these cattle becoming like Him, He means that even their feelings and emotional reactions can change to reflect His son. The Invader, when He was here on our planet, told His followers that they were to love their enemies. He explained that they were destined to be like the Enemy, who is the kind of Being who loves both the evil man and the good man. In another part of the Enemy's handbook, that troublemaker Paul promised humans they could be, in his words, "strengthened from God's glorious power, so that you may be able to pass through any experience and endure it with joy."

This inner transformation of emotions that the Enemy offers His followers is something that we must keep them blind to. Never let them realize that no one *makes* them feel angry or hurt or frustrated or miserable or lonely or abandoned or disgusted, any more than anyone *makes* them feel happy or joyful or contented or at peace. Each feeling is the human's own reaction to others or to his circumstances. When a human accepts ownership of his feelings, then and only then can he begin to deal with his feelings the Enemy's way.

Finally, as I see that our time is up for this session, one last observation. If you cannot get a human being to pay too much attention to his feelings, you may still turn a profit. In human culture, some few still believe that emotions are "unmanly" or "unspiritual." When such individuals feel emotion, encourage them to reject their feelings totally. Try to confuse feelings of anger (which the Enemy can deal with if a human faces them) with fits of rage and other active sins. Encourage such tight control in the client that emotions are pushed further and further away from his consciousness, and their very existence denied.

The fact is that at Creation the Enemy gave humans His own capacity to experience a full range of emotions. The Enemy Himself feels anger and jealousy, as well as love and compassion and the other baser emotions at which we sneer. The Enemy's goal is to shape persons who neither are ruled by their emotions nor deny them. He seeks to develop human beings who are so marked by His image that their emotional responses are in harmony with His own character. He wants them to know love and joy—but to love what He loves and rejoice at those things He values. He wants them to know anger and jealousy, but to be angry over injustice and jealous for the welfare of a brother or sister. The Enemy actually desires to enrich and deepen and fulfill the emotional potential of these disgusting creatures. And it is against such fulfillment that we fight.

So let me exhort you. Bend every effort to twist that emotional capacity all humans have to our purposes. Keep them locked in the grip of emotional immaturity. Follow the suggestions I've given you in this lecture, and believe me, you will be well on your way to the kind of success that brings us our greatest reward. And *that* is fitting humans to *our* image, twisting their emotions into shapes that generate all sorts of selfish and harmful acts. That is using human emotions in our own wise way to lead them to live out the ethics of Hell.

LECTURE FOUR

Thursday, 24 January 32913

Motivation: The Perilous Passions

In spite of wars and pestilence and famine, the human population of our planet continues to explode. Most of this explosion is occurring on continents where we have historically been able to maintain control over the destiny of individuals by shaping their society and religions. In such lands, we need only monitor a few religious and political leaders and of course the infrequent missionary. (Usually missionaries require only a minor effort on our part; we simply confuse them into identifying Christianity with Western culture. What a delight to see a missionary futilely push and pull and squeeze to make people who have no sense of time fit his idea of a "good Christian" who comes to Sunday school at 9:30 A.M. and church at 11.)

The population explosion has, however, had some impact in lands where the Enemy's Word has long been known. When you move into the field, your caseload will undoubtedly be larger than it would have been a millennium ago. You may have eight or ten clients to monitor. Since none of us is omnipresent, as the Enemy is, you will have to develop a number of special skills. One of these skills is recognizing and using human allies.

One who was a great help to me with a client was a theologian. At the time Dr. X, as we'll call him, had a psychiatric degree and was within four credits of his doctorate in theology. Yet I immediately recognized him as an ally when he sat down with my client.

This client was a young and very promising follower of the Enemy. He was what some humans term a "jock"—one of that class of human males endowed with superior athletic ability. I had turned to great advantage the success this particular young man had achieved on the basketball court. I'd carefully shaped feelings of great self-importance, had nurtured competitiveness and aggression, and of course had brought him into contact with many willing young females who were entranced by his reputation and his body.

He was being wrapped tighter and tighter by all these bonds, especially the bondage to sex, when he was converted to the Enemy camp! Unfortunately, some of the very traits I had developed were now turned against me. He valued himself so much he was convinced he would be a great warrior for his God, so he bent every effort toward holiness. In spite of his overdeveloped sex drive, he kept himself under tight control for a span of years. I was able to immobilize him part of the time with guilt over his thought life, and I encouraged a few relationships in which he slipped over the bounds he'd set for himself. But in general the situation was discouraging. Even when one month he slipped back into the old patterns and engaged in adultery, his sorrow and shame led to that disgusting confession and return of joy that King David (a similar personality type) reported in Psalm 51.

It was then that I was able to nudge my client to share his "fall" and his continuing struggles with sex with Dr. X. Ah, what glorious confusion this human ally was able to create! In the great wisdom of his "holistic approach" to life, he suggested that my client had failed to "come to grips with his humanity," that the client was looking at sexuality as something apart from masculinity, when actually it is to be integrated fully.

Dr. X pointed out that "using" a woman as a "thing" is intrinsically wrong, for a woman must be respected as a person. The relationship of a man with a woman is to be one in which affection, respect, and liking for the total person is central. Within that context sexuality is a natural part of the whole, said Dr. X, and if both choose to express their affection, respect, and liking in a sexual way, then and only then is neither "using" the other. In the context of such a relationship, sex can hardly be considered fornication.

This attractive and moral presentation by the Doctor was extremely beneficial to my client. It justified his sense of guilt by pointing out his "sin" in thinking of sexuality as something apart from personhood. It appealed to his basically decent and deep desire to value women as persons. And it also provided an ethical basis for engaging in sexual relations.

Dr. X, of course, is the very kind of human ally you will want to be alert for—someone who can provide an ethical basis for expression of those passions that humans intuitively recognize as dangerous, and yet are so strongly attracted to.

Before we go on to analysis, I want to point out a very important thing. When humans read various versions of the Enemy's handbook and come across the word *passions,* they almost immediately think "sex." The Greek word translated "passions" does *not* mean "sexual drives," although sexual drives are included. The word actually means "desires," or "longings." If we were to use the language of contemporary psychology we might say "drives," or "motives" or even "instinctive responses." Within every human, there is a whole bundle of such passions, many of which flow from the nature of humans as embodied personalities.

Because humans have a physical nature, they have such things as a sex drive, as well as needs relating to food and water. Because humans have a social nature, they have a whole set of needs related to interpersonal relationships. Because humans are (relatively) intelligent, they have certain needs to know and understand the world in which they live. Humans have a strong sense of individual self, so they have deep needs for self-realization. They need to feel and be important, to achieve, to develop their potential.

This whole bundle of personal needs, drives, desires, cravings, and motivations is encompassed in that one term *passions.* It is up to you and me, as tempters and agents of Hell, to see to it that these passions are employed to energize humans to our kind of ethical acts.

One more introductory point. In our last lecture I noted that human emotions are ethically neutral. Even the so-called negative feelings of anger or envy should not be viewed as either good or evil. A feeling may be pleasant or unpleasant, but good and evil are ethical terms and relate to actions.

It's true that some emotions do tilt a person toward actions that are evil. Humans usually associate the actions with the feelings, and that is why they have labeled the feelings themselves as "bad." But as you and I know, the most "evil" emotions are all too often the doorway to our most disastrous defeats. How glorifying it is to the Enemy (and how humiliating to us!) to see a human flush with anger, clench his fist, and then, instead of striking back, turn the other cheek. No, emotions themselves are ethically neutral. It is actions that express either the ethics of Heaven or the ethics of Hell.

Now, the same is true with human passions; they are in themselves ethically neutral. Ethics is concerned with the choices that men and women make about how their passions are expressed.

With this said, let me move on to suggest ways you and I can turn an ethical profit from human passions. Let's look at the misconceptions we want to encourage in our clients:

1. *If it is "natural" it is "right."* For the humanist in the Western Theater of Operations, where you will be assigned, the term "natural" is very significant. Once, while watching TV over a client's shoulder, I saw a young college student challenge Billy Graham's position on sex. The student argued that if he were hungry, he'd eat a ham sandwich. Hunger is natural, he said, and satisfying hunger is natural. Since sexual needs are also natural, it follows that satisfying sexual needs is acceptable.

This is of course a very ridiculous analogy. Ham sandwiches are things; human beings are persons. Using bread and meat to satisfy hunger and using another person as a piece of meat to satisfy sexual hunger are completely different things. But not too many humans will see the difference. What they will see is the parallel between the "naturalness" of the two hungers. They will often nod and repeat the argument themselves. Sex is a natural thing. So it must be all right.

Of course, this argument is never used when it comes to the completely natural need of humans to relieve themselves. Even when a human bladder is near to bursting, no respectable person thinks of urinating on a crowded city street or in a bus. The fact that elimination is *natural* can't justify the particular *way* in which the need is met. Most people accept the rules of society for eating and the rules for relieving oneself, and never argue that the rules should be broken because the activity they regulate is "natural." But you must never let them apply this common-sense notion to such issues as sex. Let them argue that, since sex is natural, *any* expression of sex or *any* approach to meeting sexual needs (short of rape) is therefore right and good.

While this simplistic approach will do for most humanists, we must use a more sophisticated approach in implanting "natural is good" thinking in the Enemy's followers. Here, like Dr. X, we need to argue from theology. Our approach may run something like this: "Other people have great worth and value to God, and must always be affirmed by us as His followers. God made humans sexual beings, so it follows that part of what it means to be fully human is to recognize and accept our sexual natures. It follows then that we must accept our own humanity (e.g., sexuality) and accept the humanity (e.g., sexuality) of others. How appropriate then to affirm our humanity and the humanity of others by expressing sexually as well as in other ways our affection, respect, liking, and valuing of one another."

It is easy to see the great attractiveness of this form of argument to the moral or religious person. On the one hand it gives them a basis to condemn promiscuity or "sex for sex's sake" as sin in others, while it makes *their own* sexual adventures moral and even religious experiences. And this—the mixed good approach to ethics—is exactly what we seek. If the human does the wrong thing (and stepping outside the Enemy's guidelines for expression of any passion is wrong) for a "good" motive, he's much less likely to realize his action is sin. And we are able to guide him into complacent bondage to the very passion he thinks he is directing toward godly goals.

I might note that the drive for self-realization can also be a very positive passion. It is rooted in the human's need to succeed—to be someone, or to accomplish something significant, or to reach his full potential. This very natural drive is something the Enemy wants to turn, in His followers, into a commitment to servant-hood. But it is something that we can twist into competitiveness and control.

This is a good passion to tap in preachers. Convince them that they must do something significant for God. Motivate them to build a bigger Sunday school, reach more homes in their communities, and have the highest percentage of conversions in their denomination. Lead them to feel they must dominate and control the church and its programs, because only they are sufficiently committed and because "God always works through one dedicated man." Soon their passion to serve significantly will have them violating all the Enemy's rules on *how* to serve . . . and they will never realize that they too have been trapped into a habit of sin by a natural passion directed toward a "good" end.

2. *Repression of passions is unhealthy.* This is again a humanistic argument that is normally related to sex. The idea is that the "natural" sexual drive not only is "good," but it requires satisfaction.

Recently this same sort of thinking has been applied to other passions. Looking out for "number one" and learning how to live a truly selfish life have been the topics of a number of recent books. (Our own Paymaster Division stimulated these books, by the way, and paid off the authors handsomely in royalties. Of course, moth and rust and inflation make even the most hand-some of such payments inadequate, as men usually discover only after they join us.) At any rate, the basic notions that a person has *a right to demand what he wants,* and that delay or denial of satisfaction of any passion is somehow "unhealthy" are major weapons in our ethical war.

This too, of course, is nonsense. The Enemy rightly describes humans who give themselves over to follow whatever course their passions demand as "like brute beasts, creatures of instinct, born only to be caught and destroyed, and like beasts they too will perish." Again, as He said, "what things they do understand by instinct, like unreasoning animals—these are the very things that destroy them."

You see, to unthinkingly follow passions involves a human being in denying, not developing, his humanity. Just as a human *has* emotions, but is more than his feelings, so a human *has* but is *more than* his passions. The natural drives and desires, the needs and longings and instinctive responses are elements of an individual's makeup, but are not his identity. As the language of the Enemy's handbook points up, animals also possess passions. But animals are bound by their natures to be controlled by their passions. Human beings, as reflections of their Creator, have been lifted above the animals.

Humans have the capacity to evaluate and judge their passions, and to choose to go or reject the way their passions lead them. The Enemy shared his own capacity to do this with humans, and it is this that sets them far above the animal creation. It is the fact that humans are by nature participants in the Eternal that makes such arguments as "if it's natural it's good" or "repression of passions is unhealthy" such utter gibberish.

If a human being truly acted on what is "natural" (that is, in accord with his essential nature) he or she would stand as judge over passions. He or she would make conscious ethical choices about when, and how, and whether or not to satisfy them. What we really mean when we encourage the argument that something is "natural" and therefore good is that men are to see themselves as mere animals, captured by their passions and forced by overwhelming inner needs to do whatever their drives demand. Our real goal is to help humans *deny* their true nature, not live by it.

If humans ever grasped the fact that they are man, not animal, they would never again suggest that "repression of passions is unhealthy." They would see that the ability to exercise control over their passions is a sign of maturity. They would see that self-control is not only an Enemy virtue; it is in fact evidence that a human has firmly grasped his true identity, and is moving toward fulfillment of his potential as a person.

But again. These are things we do not want humans to understand. And so we sow confusion. We call good evil, and evil good, and cheerfully insist that anything they want to do is natural, and that whatever is natural must be good. We convince them that repression is psychologically harmful, and so we lead them by their noses to live on instinct as the brute beasts we insist they are.

For in this the Enemy *must* be wrong. These filthy, rutting animals that muck about on our planet *cannot* have as their destiny that Eternity which the Enemy promises. They *are* animals, young fiends! One day you will be just as passionate as I am in my own deep and total commitment.

They must remain animals!

They must live as animals!

They must react as animals!

Then in the final day of our coming defeat . . . in that day they will share with us an Eternal Hell made all the more horrible for them by the fact that then too they will be racked with passions. But then, no matter how "natural" a passion may be, they will never never never never never be able to satisfy their raging desires.

HELL CENTRAL

January 24, 32913

Screwloose
Underworld University
Level 6

Dear Screwloose,

Hell Central has been monitoring your lectures since
an official charge was forwarded by Glubnose, Dean
of Faculty. You will be pleased to note that the
charge sheet was returned to Glubnose, with the di-
rective that he make no more charges until the quarter is over. In general Lower Authority is pleased
with the points you are making, although your approach
to the subject of ethics is admittedly unorthodox.

However, there is concern here about your last class.
It seems to us that you slipped into a very unseemly
emotional fit toward the end. You even lost control
enough to admit to your students that we face defeat.
Screwloose, it is our official policy never to admit
the ~~cert~~ possibility of defeat by the Enemy. We
continue to be confident that our Research Group
will come up with the Ultimate Weapon, and that somehow the Enemy's Word will be broken. You, as a senior
demon, must constantly affirm that in the end we will
somehow win.

One more thing. If you had not lost control, you
might have suggested the important strategy of whispering to human clients any time a passion is denied
or its satisfaction put off, that the discomfort of
denial is evidence the Enemy must not care for them.
"If He really loved me," we can suggest to a believer,
"He wouldn't make me go through this." Never let
humans see denial of a passion as a gift from Heaven,
designed to strengthen them and lift them up. But,
Screwloose, you know all this. Do make sure in the
future you miss no important points. . . . And, I
warn you, do not lose control again.

Kregsgelt
Kregsgelt
Department of Education
Hell Central

LECTURE FIVE

Tuesday, 29 January 32913

Belief: The Comfortable Illusion

The attendants in the mental hospital succeeded in getting the big man with the knife into the stairwell. Cautiously they followed him down to the basement level where he was trapped by locked doors. One young ward attendant sat down on the bottom step. Quietly he tried to talk the big man into giving up his knife.

"George, you know you're not Jesus Christ. Why not give me the knife, and we'll go back upstairs together?"

But George wasn't about to give up the knife, even to the attendant, who taught the Bible class on the ward every evening. Finally the other attendants got a mattress. They shielded themselves behind it, walked in on George, and took the knife away when he tried to stab them.

Most humans think the inmates of a mental hospital are people whose beliefs are illusions. Humans would be quick to point out that big George had a false belief, an "illusion" that he was the Invader. Like most humans and many demons, some of you have a tendency to measure belief by its relationship to truth. I want to suggest a rather radical notion. When we speak of psychology and of ethics, the truth or falsehood of a belief has nothing at all to do with its value to us. In fact, beliefs that are *true* may have more potential for us than those that are false! You may even want to encourage a client to just that kind of Bible study that leads him to very firm convictions about the doctrines he believes.

Let me illustrate. The young attendant who tried to talk George *out* of his belief that he was the Invader was at the same time engaged in trying to talk a fellow attendant *into* a belief that the Enemy's handbook (and thus its message) is true. Both attendants were enrolled in a nearby university; both were majoring in philosophy. My client at the time, the other attendant, was a male from a Lutheran background who had deserted his parents' faith for a thoroughgoing determinism. One evening the Christian attendant, after hours of discussion, finally challenged my client. He would *prove* that the Bible is a supernatural book.

For the next few months the two humans studied prophecy. They dug together into archeology and history to provide dates and looked at statistics and probabilities to evaluate the likelihood of biblical prophecies coming true by chance. I must say that I enjoyed this process thoroughly. How enjoyable to see their serious discussion of what could or could not be believed. At the end of the process I, as I knew I would, won a great victory.

What's that? Belglap, isn't it? You suggest that my client rejected the handbook? No, just the opposite! At the end of the process, my client was rationally convinced that it must be true. He had to admit that the only explanation for the things he had found was supernatural intervention.

Now don't look so surprised. My client's belief that the handbook is supernatural *made no change at all in his relationship with the Enemy. My client believed, but he chose not to act on his belief.*

Belief is never dangerous until one chooses to act on it. This is something the Enemy's handbook points out. "You believe that there is one God?" James asks, and then adds a rather sarcastic "Good for you. Even the demons believe that—and shudder." Then the Enemy points to faith as useless without deeds. In this He is warning His followers to take no comfort in mere mental assent to Truth. They are not to confuse *belief* with *faith. Belief* agrees that certain facts are true; *faith* commits an individual to act on what he believes.

Our essential strategy with humans is to confuse belief and faith. Thus we help humans feel comfortable because they give mental assent to what is true without ever realizing that redeeming value is to be found only in acting on beliefs. As with emotions and passions, beliefs (even "true" beliefs) are ethically neutral. Ethics is involved only when one chooses to live in opposition to or in accord with his beliefs.

Here are some practical suggestions for field operations. They are obvious, but usually overlooked by those with the kind of education you receive here at Underworld U:

1. *Keep your client's focus on the truth or falsehood of beliefs.*

By doing this, you draw his attention away from questions of how a belief might affect his life.

You will find this is relatively easy. Even human researchers know that people select their beliefs to support their prejudices. If a belief is too clearly related to a behavior change, they will reject the belief rather than change the behavior. That's why it's usually the nonsmoker who is convinced that cigarettes cause cancer, and the heavy smoker who searches for the studies put out by tobacco companies to give moral support to their policy of slow murder for profit. (Quick murder for private profit is illegal with humans. Slow murder for corporate profit is eminently respectable.)

In another human study, college students were shown a film which demonstrated that untrained collegians could really help institutionalized retarded persons. Afterwards, participants were divided into groups, and each person given a card on which to indicate whether or not he believed the message of the film. Some groups in this study were nearly unanimous in believing that collegians could help institutionalized retarded persons. But other groups who had seen the same presentation had opposite results; nearly all in these groups did *not* believe untrained collegians could help. Why the difference? Before some groups filled out their cards, a professor had announced that students could go to another room and sign up to spend two hours a week working with retarded persons in a local institution. These were the groups where members chose not to believe.

As I say, it shouldn't be hard to keep your client's attention on whether a belief is true or false. Humans don't *want* to ask the ethical question, which is, "Since I believe this, how then am I to live?" That's one reason it is so easy for us. That's why you can keep studious Christians arguing happily about prophecy and how this or that verse fits in their particular system, while blithely ignoring such conclusions of the Enemy as "since everything will be destroyed in this way, what kind of people ought you to be?"

2. *Stress the responsibility to believe correctly.* Western culture just now is more than a little suspicious of all "truth." Humans have recently adopted a very subjective approach to belief. A belief may be "all right for you," but not "all right for me." A particular moral standard may apply to some, and not to others.

Many of the Enemy's followers apply this same strange idea to outsiders, and thus hesitate to call "sin" even things that the Enemy's handbook so labels. Yet they quickly shift gears when it comes to their religion. The same person who gives a pagan freedom to believe the most obvious falsehood will quickly attack a fellow believer who differs even slightly from him in some minor point of doctrine.

This reaction is understandable. Humans have historically confused belief with faith, and assume that the more correct one's belief the more spiritual he is. So we want to stress the importance of correct belief. Let human believers think that the person who *knows* most is closest to the Enemy. (By the way. Encourage pulpit committees to place priority on a pastoral candidate's academic background. And whisper that a candidate who can argue convincingly in favor of every point and subpoint in their ten-page doctrinal statement must surely be God's man for the church.)

Of course, this approach differs from the approach to selecting spiritual leaders given in the Enemy's handbook. A leader is to be "apt to teach," but the focus is placed by the Enemy on his *practice* of sound doctrine. A spiritual leader is, as I recall, to be no striker (the Enemy wants to replace competitiveness with wishy-washy cooperation). The human leader is to be gentle, to be freed from materialism, to have self-control, and so on.

You see the danger. The person in whom the Enemy delights and who makes us a strong antagonist is the Christian who concentrates on a *faith* approach to the Enemy's handbook. He concentrates on putting what he learns and believes into practice. In our warfare with the Enemy and His hosts we can usually ignore the person who concentrates on *what* to believe; he usually misses the more significant issue of *how* to believe.

This, by the way, is sure to be misunderstood by humans, so you can even permit individuals to raise this issue. Anyone who suggests that *how* to believe (that is, how a believer is to hold to and use the Enemy's Word) is ultimately more important than *what* to believe (that is, than building a more and more accurate understanding of the content of the Enemy's Word) is sure to be attacked by other humans. They will assume such a person is saying "what we believe is unimportant." They will attack him violently for his low view of Scripture. And they will never stop to wonder how humans in earlier ages, who had less truth, could be so highly commended by the Enemy. Noah, who knew little about eschatology or hamarteology, received praise from God for his faith. Abraham had just a verbal promise to hold on to. Yet, in spite of the fact that he could not discourse on the Order of

Decrees, or quote John 3:16, or explain why the Rapture occurs before rather than after tribulation, Abraham is still identified in the Bible as the model for all men who have faith.

To say that *how* men believe is more important than *what* they believe is simply to say that God asks humans to respond with trust and obedience to what He has shown them. He does not ask them to master every verse of the Bible. Since this is what He wants, what *we* want is a generation of Christians who care passionately about *what* they and others believe, but never trouble themselves with questions about whether they live what they learn.

3. *Encourage pride in "correct theology."* For some strange reason, humans take pride in intelligence. You can tell this is a vulnerable point by listening to young mothers. They never say, "My Joey is so emotional," or "My Susan has such fine passion." Oh no. What they say is, "My child is so *smart!*"

The same kind of thing continues as children grow. Parents brag about grades. Smarter teens complain about the dumb ones. In college and after, "He made Phi Beta Kappa," said in tones of suitable awe, tells us that humans place high value on knowing. Why, there's an organization called Mensa, whose membership is limited to those with IQs in the top 2 percent of the nation.

These things provide clues for an alert demon. If humans take pride in superior knowledge, why then, let's encourage believers to be proud about what *they* know. When we stimulate pride in *anything* we build solid barricades against the Enemy. When we stimulate pride in correct belief, we gain even more. We cut a Christian off from other disciples of the Enemy who do not believe exactly as he does. We establish false criteria for measuring the contribution of others; in many congregations there are those who have spiritual insights but are disregarded because they don't "know" as much as others. And yes, we gain many benefits playing the natural tendency of humans to exalt knowledge. You surely want to encourage them to be proud of their correct beliefs.

One word of warning. That meddler Paul in one of his letters spoke of knowledge "puffing up." He contrasts knowledge with love, which he says "builds up." Be sure that your human clients feel that truth has priority over love. Let them feel sure they are willing to love anyone—anyone who is committed to the truth as they understand it, so there will be some "basis for fellowship." Fight with your full strength any suggestion that the Enemy's followers are called to love even those who do not yet believe as they do. Love does build up, and as the barriers are broken down, they might discover how sinful it is to take pride in their own grasp of the Enemy's Truth, which is far too vast for any human mind to begin to encompass.

Oh yes. One more suggestion. If any client of yours should happen to stumble on the principles I've shared in this class, whisper a verse from the Enemy's handbook. Remind them, "The Bible says be transformed by the renewing of your mind." They will assume that this means filling the mind with correct instead of incorrect beliefs.

Never let them find out that the Greek word in this verse which is translated "mind" means "way of thinking," not "storage bin." The Enemy desires that these creatures, in which He takes such perverted pride, treat His handbook as a resource. He wants them to let His Word shape their view of all things. That "renewal of the mind" concerns application rather than storage of His truth is clear from the rest of the Bible passage: "Then you will be able to put to the test and to prove the will of God, which is [He says] good and perfect and pleasing."

The mind the Enemy seeks is a mind that focuses on *doing* Truth. We demons don't mind if they "believe" right things. The Enemy's Word is like a flashlight. If humans just stare into it, it is useless to them, and they'll stumble harmlessly in the dark. But if they point the Word at their path . . . ah, then we are in trouble. For He designed the things they treat as "beliefs" to be Light, to make clear the issues and decisions they face as they walk through life.

You see, what humans believe *is* less of an issue than how they believe. As I said at the beginning of this lecture, the truth or falsehood of a belief may have little to do with how neatly we can turn it to our advantage. You can even use the Enemy's own Word to advantage—certainly Our Father Below used it that way in the Garden of Eden. To make good use of His Word, remember the basic principles I have suggested today. Focus human attention on whether a belief is true or false. Don't let them ask how their beliefs should affect their lives. Urge clients to insist that everyone they know be "doctrinally correct." And build on that foundation good healthy pride in their own set of beliefs.

Follow these rules, and you'll shatter fellowships, reinforce divisive barriers, and keep clients from having renewed minds that grasp His truth in ways that are dangerous to us all.

LECTURE SIX

Thursday, 31 January 32913

Will: Practical Paralysis

We are coming to the end of the first section of our course on the ethics of Hell. In this section I have shown ways that each facet of the human psyche may be played by us to paralyze the one faculty we fear. The will.

By the way, I've been informed that I must give examinations. At the end of the hour I'll pass out a short test. I expect as soon as I turn my back that you, as any follower of Our Father Below, will cheat. Please do. This is a course in ethics, and I much prefer you engage in ethical actions than intellectual exercise.

Now. A brief review.

I have suggested that we must view ethics as a practical rather than theoretical discipline. Ethics deals with the choices humans actually make in their "real world." The traditional approach to ethics is to treat it as a branch of philosophy. This assumes that since one who knows good will do it, a study of ethics should concentrate on knowing. I, however, have taken a different approach. I've suggested that the ethics of Hell is best served by approaching ethics from a psychological point of view. You and I, as agents of Hell, have many resources within the human personality we can use to lead clients to follow our kind of ethical behavior. To understand these resources and then to manipulate them is the key to what the Enemy Scriptures call our "devices."

So in this course we've scanned several psychological systems a particular deception might engage. We've seen how vulnerable these brutes are to manipulation of their perception of themselves, their emotions, their passions, and their beliefs. But note: *Every manipulation is designed to the same end—The Paralysis of Their Will.* Feelings and passions and beliefs are not in themselves ethically good or evil. Good and evil are terms that in ethics can only be applied to the choices and actions that may flow from such inner struggles. Thus our whole goal is to cut these cattle off from that act of faith in which they choose and try to do the Enemy's will.

This is the absolute heart of Enemy ethics. He seeks an obedient response to Himself and His will. A human's emotions may scream with fear, his passions may pull him away, his muddled thinking may distort, but let him in even a stumbling way step out to act in faith, and we lose while our hated Enemy wins.

In His scribblings, the Enemy puts the issue this way: "Today, if you should hear His Voice, do not harden your heart." In that passage the Enemy clearly links unbelief with disobedience, and faith with obedience. Those who truly trust express their faith in obedience. So it is this perverse thing of obedient response to the Voice of God that we always battle.

Let me say it again. Our ethical battle is always mounted *against obedient response* to the Enemy. We use many many means, and manipulate every faculty of the human personality. But the sole end we have in view is to keep human beings from the choice to obey.

Thus, fiends, the *will*, more than any other human faculty, is the ethical key. I realized this early in my own career. But I did not realize that, even when a human makes a decision, all is not lost. At first I would panic when a human I was guiding would grit his teeth and mutter, "I *will* live for the Lord." My mistake was to confuse the inner decision, "I will," for obedience itself. Actually, there is a vast difference. Such choices are much like emotions or passions. They exist *inside* the human client. As long as they remain inside and are not translated into actions, they are neither dangerous to us nor pleasing to the Enemy.

Later, as I became more and more familiar with these brutes we herd, I realized how foolish it was to assume that once a human made a "decision" he would go on to act on it. Like New Year's Resolutions, most human decisions are made to be broken, not acted on.

This gives us a key for our strategy. When dealing with the human will, try to keep a human from realizing that he needs to make any decision at all. But if he does make a decision, then try to stretch out as long as possible the time between the decision and acting on the decision. Usually you can stretch the time out so long the human will never notice that his decision hasn't affected his lifestyle; you can keep him complacently pleased with himself for his willingness to respond to God.

Here are a few practical hints for implementing this strategy:

1. *Confuse intentions with action.* Someone once observed that "the road to hell is paved with good intentions." I believe one nightclub (as humans used to call their discotheques before lights and loud music were added), actually was called "Hell," and had various appropriate sayings painted on its steps: "I'll do it tomorrow," "I plan to spend more time with my family," "I will stop drinking," "I'll turn off the TV at ten," and a few others.

That "good intentions" saying is so familiar that everyone laughs and passes it off. (This, by the way, is a very successful strategy developed by our Linguistics Task Group. We make significant truths seem puerile by encouraging their use as "sayings." Such "sayings" become so familiar that even "Jesus loves me" is smiled at indulgently today as something young children sing in spiritual infancy.)

But we recognize how terribly stark and brutally accurate sayings may be. "The road to hell is paved with good intentions" is a totally revealing expression of one of our major strategies. Yet by making humans overfamiliar with it, as an old and clever joke, we have been able to defuse its insight.

The point is this. A decision to do something *tomorrow* is not harmful to us, and may be helpful. And humans are very open to a suggestion to do *anything* "tomorrow." "I'll diet tomorrow" is extended day by day into an infinite regression of tomorrows, and leads to weight gain instead of loss. "I'll start jogging tomorrow" excuses today's shortness of breath, but never leads to restoring a battered heart or stretching sagging lungs. Only if the overweight person pushes back from the table and says firmly, "No pie for me, thank you" is the decision to diet meaningful. A change comes only if a potential jogger says, "No elevator for me this morning. I'm going to walk up the two flights of stairs to my office." It is the decision to do something small *now,* rather than to begin something big *tomorrow,* that makes a difference in weight or health.

The ethical situation is exactly parallel. Let a human plan to start a special Bible course at evening school the next fall. But don't let him put down his *Reader's Digest* to pick up a new version of the Enemy handbook now. Encourage a father to plan a significant vacation next summer. But keep him from taking five minutes to talk with his child about school tonight. You'll find ways to keep him from signing up for the class when fall comes. You'll find a way to block the summer vacation when spring arrives. Don't focus your attention on the distant future. Let your human client make his plans and dream his dreams; just be sure that he keeps on confusing his good intentions with ethical action, and everything will be all right.

2. *Convince him that he cannot act significantly . . . yet.* From our point of view, big decisions about plans for the future are much to be preferred over small actions taken now. If your human client ever notices that, in spite of his intentions, his life is not changing, you have a very effective fallback. In such cases, simply point out that your client has no opportunity to do something significant now. But when he does, well. . . .

I once had a client who was always talking about what he would do if he had a million dollars. He had it all planned: this mission would be given so much, that ministry of his church would be funded, the needs of the poor in his community would be met through that other project. My client often thought it was such a shame he was poor, because if he had money, he would certainly use it for the Enemy's glory.

I was able to keep this client's thoughts so focused on what he would do if he had millions that he never did evaluate how he used the thousands he did have. I kept him in a pretty state of debt through all those wonderful credit cards humans issue these days. Never in all the years I was with him did he ever stop to ask, "If I *don't* buy this new color TV, what might I do with the money?" I recall him and his wife talking for days about the color and style of a new rug for their living room, and never ever wondering aloud if they needed the new rug, or how the money might be used by those missions they dreamed about supporting when they became rich.

Actually, in almost every demon/client relationship you will find opportunities to use this device. Teenagers are convinced that they cannot make any significant decisions while they live in their parents' homes, but every day they do decide how to use those twenty-four hours the Enemy allots each individual. A man will wish he had been called to the mission field so he could evangelize Africans, and never think of inviting pagan neighbors over for a meal. Some women will wish they were men so they could "have a ministry," and never realize that standing behind a pulpit is only one of many ways to communicate the Enemy's Word.

Ah yes. The more you can make a client focus on the limitations of his or her situation, the less each will see the opportunities for obedient response the Enemy gives every human. The two little words, "if only," are great ammunition for us in our invisible war.

3. *Keep decisions general and not specific.* To save time for that quiz, I must make this lecture brief. So just one more point. Let your clients make all the big decisions they wish. Big decisions are nearly always vague and general. By "big" I mean things like "I will commit my whole life to God." And "I surrender my business to you, Lord." And "I will become a missionary if you want me."

At first glance big decisions seem dangerous. But only at first glance. Here again we are dealing with an *internal* human operation. Again too we are dealing with the future. And with big decisions we have an added benefit. We have decisions that are so amorphous and difficult to define that the decision often carries no implications of specific action.

What we fear is the little decision that says, when confronted with an embarrassing question, "I will tell you the truth *now.*" What we fear is the businessman who asks "What is honoring to God?" when he makes a daily operations decision. What we hate is the "future missionary" who determines to equip himself by staying home to study *tonight.*

But again, don't fret. Humans make our task easy for us. They are the ones who label general issues "big" and specific issues "little." They are easily confused, and seldom grasp the obvious fact that little decisions deal with the reality of their lives, while big decisions are essentially unreal. The big decision only becomes real when it is applied to guide choices day by day.

Humans cannot change their pasts. They can look ahead, but they can never act out their future. The only time that a human has in which to choose or to do *anything* is the time that is present to him. That's why I say that, for humans, past and future are not real issues. That's why the only decisions humans make which can harm us are decisions which concern present acts.

The Enemy knows this too, of course, and has warned them in His handbook. "Why all this stress on behavior?" He says in one place. "Because, as I think you have realized, the present time is of the highest importance." It is in present time that a human's life is lived, and his ethics expressed in action. It is in present time that the human will must operate, choosing *now* acts which set the course of his future life.

And so we clearly see the mission we agents of Hell have been given. It is to render humans ineffectual in their present, to paralyze their will to act in the Now. It matters little, class, how you accomplish this mission. Use their emotions. Use their distorted images of themselves. Use their drives and motivations. Use their beliefs. Use even their wills, encouraging them to make big decisions about what they will do in their future. But whatever you do, keep humans from looking to the Enemy and asking the fatal question, "What do You want me to do *now?*"

If they ask Him that, He will show them.

And then, if they respond in faith, expressed as obedience, a promising meal of polluted and rotting humanity crawls out of our cooking pots and stumbles toward health and wholeness . . . and Him.

Ethics of Hell
Professor Screwloose
Spring Quarter, 32913

Quiz One

True/False: Fill in each blank with a T or an F.

_____ 1. Comfortable sins are better than those which prick the conscience.

_____ 2. The person who knows good will usually do it.

_____ 3. Human good intentions please the Enemy.

_____ 4. Sinful emotions always lead to sinful actions.

_____ 5. Human needs are natural, and therefore evil.

_____ 6. Humans "are what they believe."

_____ 7. True beliefs are more dangerous to us than false beliefs.

_____ 8. The ethics of Heaven seeks to stimulate a response of faith/obedience from humans.

_____ 9. Because the human will is sinful, a human cannot choose to respond to the Enemy.

_____ 10. We demons should do all we can to keep humans away from the Enemy's handbook.

Essay: Write not more than three lines about four of the following:

1. Explain one strategy demons use with human emotions.

2. Explain one strategy demons use with human beliefs.

3. Explain one strategy demons use with human motivations.

4. Explain one strategy demons use with human wills.

5. Explain how human emotions are not "real."

6. Explain how a human's perception of himself as weak can be used by demons.

7. Explain why ethics does not relate to "good" or "bad" motives.

8. Explain how true beliefs can be turned to demonic advantage.

9. Explain why the ethics of Heaven is focused on the "now" experiences of a human, while the ethics of Hell focuses on the future.

10. If you were a human, which of Satan's devices would you be most susceptible to?

PART II

The Language of Ethics:
The Power of Words

Department of Temptry

February 1, 32913

Screwloose
Visiting Faculty
Underworld University
Level 6

Dear Screwloose:

I cannot express my relief! Your distorted "psychology of ethics" section is finished! I twitched in
pure disgust at the drivel you presented to your students. Such academically trivial material will, I
assure you, soon be forgotten. And when I return
to UU I will personally eradicate every record of
your . . . your meanderings.

Thank Beelzebub that the next section of your course
is traditional. How refreshing it will be to review
the erudite analyses of the great thinkers of the
ages of such ethically significant concepts as Law,
Freedom, Authority, Truth (pardon the expression),
and so on. I trust that you will visit our library,
and explore the vast reserves of knowledge stored
there.

Perhaps, if this next section of your course is even
slightly respectable, I will be restrained in the
actions I have planned to take on my return. So
please accept this as a word of encouragement to do
better. And as a warning.

Glubnose

Glubnose
Dean of Faculty (on leave)

 UNDERWORLD UNIVERSITY

February 4, 32913

Glubnose
Very Junior Observer
Level 14

Poor old Glubnose,

You still don't understand, do you? Why, you boob,
I see now why our ages-long battle with the Enemy
has gone so poorly, in spite of our many superiorities
over humans. It is because idiots like you have been
placed in charge of training our hordes.

I have no intention at all of engaging in scholarly
analysis of ethical terms. I leave that to you,
with all those dusty books of yours in the library.
They can rest there for Eternity for all I care.
You can be sure none of my class will crack them
either, to muddle their thinking as yours is by "much
learning."

What do I intend for this next section of the course?
No philosophical analysis, but an examination of common usage. You see, Glubnose, it is not the abstract
notions of philosophers that shape the choices of the
common man (99.999 percent of all humans). In fact,
it is the unnoticed connotations that attach themselves to ethical terms without men being aware that
form the essence of the ethics of Hell. A twist
here, a turn there, and a perfectly good word can
be turned to pernicious advantage by a demon who has
some sensitivity to the power of words over human
beings.

Oh no. I assure you, Glubnose, I will not turn now
to the traditional. I am a practical demon, not one
of your philosophers. As for your threats, do your
worst. I assume they will be as ineffective as everything else you've tried these last few centuries.

Most sincerely,

Screwloose

(Professor) Screwloose

LECTURE SEVEN
Tuesday, 5 February 32913

Law: The Stone God

Before we begin this new section of our course, let me comment on your exam papers. Generally, I was pleased. Several of you demonstrated a good grasp of what I was saying—something I don't expect after years in the University have dulled your thinking. However, whatever grade you received, don't let it go to your heads. The grade means nothing. What you do on the field is the only true test of learning.

I will, however, return your papers, with an answer key posted outside my office door.*

Now, then, let's begin this next section of our study of the Ethics of Hell—the practice of distorting human choices to fit them for our Eternal company.

Our theme is the power of words. What you must remember as we discuss words is that human thought processes are characteristically muddled and confused. They use words in imprecise ways. Words that to you or me have stark and unmistakable meaning will be cloudy and distorted for them. At times we are even able to turn the meaning of words around completely, so that humans will take them to mean the opposite of what they really say. Thus we are able to have humans adopt such phrases as "for mature audiences only" whenever they deal with sex in an adolescent way, and get them to speak of bondage to their passions as "liberation."

But the greatest work we can do for Our Father Below is to sow confusion about truly significant ethical terms. We do this not by focusing on what words denote (their "meaning") but by focusing on what words connote (a host of unexpressed notions that stick to a word like mud to a farmer's boots). It is the muddied meaning of

---

*Note: A copy of the answer key was obtained and is included as Appendix A on page 164.

words we want to encourage, for it is through the muddied meanings that we shape the reactions and choices of humans.

For instance, in recent decades we've helped many react positively to the muddied meaning of the word *law*. Some ethnic and racial groups have seen "law and order" as code words for oppression and brutality. Some politicians manipulate these terms to gain votes from those who *want* oppression. And thousands of young people have come to view every law, from those of the nation to the laws of God, as props for an establishment they reject.

Ah yes. When we muddy the meaning of the great words that hold human societies together, we make great gain.

My goal in this section of my lectures, then, is to show you how to use the muddied meaning of critical words for Our Father's benefit. And, of course, for our own delight. Now then, let's get on with our first word: *law*.

Human Law

You'd think any idiot would realize that law is essential to humans. Laws will always be developed whenever any two humans live within miles of one another. The Greeks, to whom they trace the common New Testament word for law, realized that social life always requires commonly recognized rules of conduct. In that sense, customs were looked on as laws. Human laws are simply practices which are commonly agreed on by a society as the "right" way to regulate life.

Now, humans always need such customs for the simple reason that otherwise they would never agree on anything. Picture if you will two women setting the first table, and arguing which side of the plate to set the fork. Then picture their husbands, sitting down and looking at the array as they wonder, "Which of these blasted things does she want me to use for the salad?" Well, humans solve problems like these by developing customs, and they even write books on "rules of etiquette" to guide table behavior.

It's the same with any human relationships. Bankers set up codes of written or unwritten rules telling to whom they can loan money and to whom they cannot. (The general rule they follow is, never loan money to someone who doesn't already have more than he needs . . . unless he is a director of the bank.) Banking rules provide a whole set of accepted customs that in time take on the force of law, and give very strict procedures bankers must follow to legally foreclose on a widow's acre.

Even the human judicial system relies on custom, encrusted as tradition, and finally canonized as "precedent," to define right and wrong behavior. But the key issue is this: *As long as everyone recognizes and accepts the rules of a society, human law functions to hold that society together, and to give a sense of security to the individual.* He knows how to "play the game" because he knows the rules. An individual may not keep the rules, but even if he breaks them he knows the penalty he must pay, for this too has been defined by the laws and customs of his society.

But there is a problem with human law. Customs and traditions, and the laws that grow out of them, are shaped in *changing* societies. What was appropriate at the turn of the century may not, because of different conditions, be appropriate now. So humans are always, except in the most stagnant of societies, caught in a strange tension with law. On the one hand, humans struggle to hold onto law and custom and tradition, because these provide security by defining right and wrong. On the other hand, progress pressures humans to reevaluate their laws and customs and traditions to meet the challenge of changing conditions.

In some decades, this tension produces rebels. A whole generation becomes frustrated by the unresponsiveness of tradition to changes that need to be made. In other decades, this tension produces reactionaries. A generation is frightened by the rush of events, and demands a return to the tried and true values of the past.

The Greek philosophers were aware that even the best of human customs are fallible. So some sought a cosmic, universal law. If only men could be in harmony with the universe itself, they argued, then a man might find peace of mind even in spite of chaos. Of course, the search for a universal law never troubled most people. As always, the majority then simply assumed that their customs and traditions *were* expressions of universal law. If someone offended against custom (as the early Christians did in their peculiar ideas about not worshiping idols or performing other patriotic duties), such a person was labeled ungodly. Pure moral indignation was more than enough to incite whole populations against these "Christian" tradition breakers. Whatever the tradition of a time, it is unthinkingly accepted by most people as being *really* right, and by all who hold some other notion as being *really* wrong.

Before we move on to look at the introduction of Enemy law into history, I want to make a few practical points. There are definitely ways that we can use the peculiarities of human law to muddy the thinking of the Enemy's people and channel their energies into futility:

1. Remember that it is always to our benefit to confuse human customs with the Enemy's rights and wrongs. For instance, for a few hundred years the Enemy's followers have been meeting on Sunday mornings. Recently a number of His disciples have started again to meet at other times, and called these other meetings "church" even though some take place in homes. This has raised the wrath of the traditionalists. To them "church" is something that happens in a special building between 9:30 and 12 noon Sunday morning. So today the two groups have a delightful time battling each other about the "right" time and place to meet as the Invader's Church.

Wonderful! How encouraging to see such moral indignation and such angry attacks mounted by the Enemy's followers on each other, while they ignore us and the real war. You see how well it serves us to lift this mere custom—and a young one at that!—to the level at which breaking the custom seems as serious as breaking the Enemy's law. (And please, young fiends, never let the battlers look into church history and find out that the first time of meeting was evening!)

2. Where we can't lift human customs to give them as much or more force than the Enemy's law, then try the reverse strategy. Make humans feel the changeless principles of revealed Law are as open to reinterpretation as human customs! Human customs *must* be evaluated by situations. Human customs have to be responsive to situations, and changes must constantly be worked into their framework. A human who takes this open and courageous view, who can live with the risk of change, can often be encouraged to carry change *too far.* He can be encouraged to challenge basic realities revealed by the Enemy, and be encouraged to battle for changes in the very Word itself.

Soon, to be responsive to the demands of women's liberation, he will be muttering prayers to a Father/Mother God, or leading campaigns for the ordination of homosexual clergy, and insisting that a "theology of liberation" justifies killing thousands in South America so a new social order that "respects human life" can be imposed.

Yes, if we cannot raise human traditions in their minds to the status of unchangeable divine law, then let's lower unchangeable divine law to the status of changeable human traditions.

3. There is one final point I'd like to make. In general, *the less significant morally a human custom or tradition is, the more ferociously a religious person will defend it.* And, I should add, the more ferociously he or she will attack a fellow believer who violates the custom.

That Sunday morning rule of theirs is a good example. Why, in His guidebook the Enemy has even said explicitly that His people have freedom to choose the days and times they set aside to honor Him. Even a moment's thought should convince anyone that it is what happens when the Church of the Enemy meets—the prayers, the feasting on His Word, the exhortation and support and encouragement they give each other to follow Him—that is important. These are the things the Enemy cares about . . . and that we care about spoiling. But fortunately, Sunday-morning-onlyites don't stop to think, and instead play into our hands by being upset (and frightened) by those who break their custom.

Yes, let's major on the minor issues of Christian faith and life. Let's convince the religious among our clients that a man's relationship with God can be measured by whether or not he drinks a glass of wine with his meal, or goes to movies, or does something equally insignificant in the Enemy's sight. Let's make the little customs loom larger than the significant law of love and mercy, and we will do Our Father's work well.

Divine Law

Let me make a few comments on the nature of divine law, and then move quickly to how we subvert it.

Unlike changing human customs, the law which the Enemy revealed is rooted in eternity. It is, in fact, an expression of His own terrifying character. Just as you or I would find delight in giving a law that demands a man take bloody revenge for any slight (a law which would express our own nature and pride), so the Enemy took delight in giving a Law that counsels forgiveness, because that law expresses His character. "Don't commit adultery," He says, because He holds faithfulness as an abiding value. "Don't murder," He says, because He prizes the lives of those slugs. His law, then, is first of all an expression of His own character, and it is for this reason that His law stands outside of time and change, to judge all human societies. His Law was written in stone, because it does not change.

There are other implications of the Enemy's choice of stone for the writing of His Law. Stone is the antithesis of life. There is no warmth, no yielding, no pulsing motion in stone as there is in any form of animal life. Even the tiniest living cell is in constant motion—feeding, growing, reproducing, changing. But stone. Ah, stone stands in contrast to the constant flux; it is unaffected, unyielding, cold. Stone laws cannot be bent. Instead, living things who dash themselves against them are crushed and shattered.

The Enemy's character was translated into stone in order that humans might look up and see *righteousness* looming above them in its most awesome form. Stone law was given to help mankind realize that, judged by God's changeless standards, every human crouches guilty before Him. So the Enemy's handbook says "by the law is the knowledge of sin," and "whatever law says, it says to those who are under the law, that every mouth may be stopped, and the whole world become guilty before God."

Law is God's moral character expressed in stone, so that every human pretension to righteousness might be crushed. These facts have great implications for humans—which we never want them to even glimpse. Never let them realize that God Himself is not stone. Or that God does not seek to crush humans, but to lift them up beside Himself! Never let them wonder whether God might have some way *other than law* for His character to find living expression. Never let them puzzle about how God intends for them to experience the righteousness expressed in stone without being crushed.

I'll speak more of this later. But now, let me impress this on you. One of our greatest resources is the very law that the Enemy has given—with its purpose and function twisted and changed. We found this approach very effective in dealing with Israel. God entered into a covenant relationship with Israel: He would be their God, and they would be His people. But we were able to make Israel view its special status as a privilege dependent on obedience to law, rather than due to God's promise. Law assumed a dominant role in Israel; it became the mediator between God and man. It became the way in which one of God's true people was distinguished from another.

Thus we were able to cause Israel to turn from the Enemy. They turned from the faithfulness and forgiveness expressed in His covenant promises, and began to worship a stone god. We succeeded in making the stones appear to *be God!*

This is a beautiful example of how we pervert and use the law. We lead the religious to worship the stone god as the way to spiritual deliverance or growth. And what benefits we receive!

In those who succeed in keeping part of the law, we create pride and self-righteousness. They look at persons who are weaker than they and feel so self-satisfied. By keeping the letter of some law they think they have achieved *all* that the Enemy requires—and never realize that truly keeping the whole law demands that they be totally like the Person whose character the stones (imperfectly) express!

We achieve the benefit of creating despair. A human tries to please the stone god, and finds himself falling short. He tries again and fails. In his failure, because his eyes are fixed on unyielding law, he loses hope. "I can't . . ." he sobs, and sinks in the dust, as we gloat.

We achieve the benefit of judging. The person who takes pride in the ways he conforms to law condemns others who do not. He pulls back from the unbeliever who curses, because he himself is not "that kind of person." For his weaker brothers he has contempt or pity, but never compassion.

We achieve the benefit of endless guilt that saps a human's strength and destroys his will to try. Law brings the crushing knowledge of failure, and so creates a guilt that law itself has no answer for. Keep a human worshiping the stone god, and he will never realize that the Enemy's purpose is not to underline guilt but to provide forgiveness.

And another glorious benefit. We build a sense of compulsion. You see, the stone god of law demands, insists, threatens, commands, restricts, and compels. A man or woman who worships the stone god always senses a demand to be or to do something that he or she is not. "I can't" wages constant war with "you must," until anger or frustration overcomes hope and creates resentment against God's "unreasonable demands."

And there lies our victory. If we can lead men to worship the stone god, the impossible demands of an unyielding law will surely lead them to turn away from the Enemy, who never intended to be worshiped as stone. Law always shouts at men, "You must!" But men cannot! As long as we keep mankind's eyes on law, there is no way out of that dilemma. "You must" echos in their minds, till some deceive themselves and pretend "I do," while others crumble and admit "I don't," and still others scream back, "I won't!"

Whenever the stone god is mistaken for the Enemy, all those benefits are ours. Now, one final word of warning. What we do *not* want is the believer who comes *casually* to law. He sees the stone expressions of righteousness, and rather than being crushed or moved to frantic self-effort, he simply says, "Of course."

"Of course God is that kind of Person."

And then he turns away from the stone god to the Enemy. In simple faith he says, "Father, I need to be more like You. Write Your character on my heart."

When *that* happens, the stone god is set back in the niche the Enemy originally carved for it. When that happens, the Enemy *will* write on the living personality of His follower that vital righteousness of His own personality. When that happens, the words of Paul come true and "the righteous requirements of the law [are] fully met" by humans who do not "live according to the sinful nature but according to the Spirit." That glance at Law, that recognition of the Enemy's character, and turning to seek Him . . . that is something we must guard against in His followers.

Actually, all the Enemy's followers were first of all slain by law. They recognized their guilt when they stood under its condemnation. But then they looked to the Invader, and saw the promise of forgiveness in His cross. The torn flesh and flowing blood of the Invader spoke louder of forgiveness than the stones did of sin. Turning to Him, they were given a righteousness that they could never attain and that we, in spite of aeons of research, cannot understand. When that happened, the Enemy's purpose for law in their lives was fulfilled. Now these vermin are invited to come boldly to Him, to find the mercy and the grace they need to live out the righteousness they have been given.

And this we cannot abide! This we will not *permit*. We grab their ears, and jerk their heads around again, and point them back to law. "Worship your stone god," we whisper. "Look at law, and away from Calvary." Sinai, not Golgotha, *must* fill their sight.

LECTURE EIGHT
Thursday, 7 February 32913

Freedom: The Fleeting Fantasy

Humans have a great capacity to muddy the meaning of ethical terms. We, of course, are dedicated to splattering them even more liberally. Between us and them, the moral realities are well disguised. Last Tuesday I outlined something of how the meaning of *law* is muddied by mankind. Today I want to focus on the term *freedom*.

Well, what does the stone god of law have to do with freedom? Ah, you see, the two are intimately linked. That's why I began this section of the course with a lecture on *law*. It is when men accept law as God, and feel the oppression of its incessant demands, that they most yearn for "freedom." When men sense law as compulsion, rather than simply a stone marker set along the road to point the way to Calvary, they desire the kind of freedom we want them to demand: a "freedom" that exists only in their imaginations—a fleeting fantasy.

Law revealed righteousness to all mankind. Law expresses righteousness in demanding terms. "Thou shalt not" is absolute, compelling. Humans who look at the Enemy's law sense that compulsion and the demand it places on them. Some immediately rebel and shout out, "I want freedom! I want to be free from outside compulsion, free to do what *I* want to do when I want to do it!"

This is the muddied meaning of *freedom*—the idea of freedom as "freedom *from*."

This isn't hard to understand. Even when ethics isn't involved, freedom is usually perceived as freedom *from* some outside compulsion. The teenager wants freedom from his parents' rules so he can stay out as late as he wants, or eat whatever junk food he chooses. The poor person wants freedom from his poverty, and imagines that wealth would loose him from all bonds. The

77

cripple wants freedom from his wheelchair, to be able to run and leap and dance. Even politically, the word *freedom* refers to acts of governments that citizens view as oppressive. Freedom *of the press* means freedom *from* government control and coercion. Some today even push the concept to mean freedom from any obligation to provide the courts with evidence of crime. It's no wonder that *freedom* in human thinking seems to require a release from an outer compulsion, and an unrestricted opportunity to do as one pleases.

Now, it suits us perfectly to encourage this notion of freedom. It suits us perfectly to apply this notion of freedom to ethics and morality. And we have done some excellent work in this area.

In sexual ethics we have gotten humans to apply the word *liberated* to an individual who commits a constant string of adulteries. Humans today praise such people as "free" from the "hang-ups" that old-fashioned morality has caused. We've applied the same term to "gay liberation," insinuating that homosexuals should be "free" to practice their "sexual preference" as an "acceptable alternative lifestyle." (Of course, gays have always been "free" to practice their interesting perversion. What they really want is for other humans to agree that they are *right* to do so.)

So it's no wonder that humans speak of "freedom" whenever they want to excuse doing things they know are wrong. How exciting it is for us when they muddy the meaning of freedom until they believe that freedom means the right to do wrong!

This is the relationship between *law* and *freedom,* as we use the terms in our ethics of Hell. *Law* means unreasonable and frustrating demands. *Freedom* means approval when we do what law reveals to be wrong.

When we can trap a human into confusing his decision to sin with being free, then we have truly achieved. We have connected a positive term with a negative act, so that humans feel it is actually good to be bad.

True Freedom

The fact of the matter is, humans are never free. Every human lives a life compressed by inner and outer restraints. Each has the same limited number of hours in a day. Each needs approximately the same amount of sleep. Even those with unlimited supplies of money are limited in what they can spend it on. What good would it be to buy all the food in the world? A human who gorged himself could only eat so much—and hasten his death in the process. A human who drank only the finest wines and liquors could drink only so much, and then would fall into insensibility while his liver turned to shoe leather.

No, the very nature of humans as finite beings is that they are limited and never really "free." A human can do "anything he wants" only within limitations. He wants to fly like Superman? He can jump off a roof. But if he does, he will certainly fall. He is free to jump, but not free to change the laws of gravity.

As we know, it is the same with ethics and morality. Humans can exercise their "freedom" to sin . . . but they can never avoid the consequences. They are free to choose evil, but not free to choose evil *safely*. They are not even free to choose evil *comfortably*. The Enemy has revealed righteousness in external law and has also planted a witness to goodness inside human personalities. They laugh at out-of-date morality, but their consciences accuse them. That is why they fasten so quickly on "freedom" to describe their ways. They must have some acceptable "good" to excuse them for choosing what they know to be wrong.

Really, the idea that freedom is "freedom from" anything is a very fleeting fantasy. But the fact that they are *never* free from limitations imposed on them by the outside world and by their own inner natures is something we do not want them to consider.

Nor do we want them to discover the freedom Heaven gives. The Enemy points out that no humans can choose between unlimited opportunities to do whatever they want. The choice humans have is to select *which restrictions* they will be slaves to. The Enemy calls them outright to become "slaves of righteousness." Willingly submit, He asks. And He warns them against becoming "slaves to sin." Explaining that choice, the Enemy's book says, "When you offer yourselves to someone to obey him as slaves, you are slaves to the one whom you obey—whether you are slaves to sin, which leads to death, or to obedience, which leads to righteousness."

When a follower of the Enemy chooses to do wrong, he becomes the slave of the sin he has chosen. That sin *will* have its impact in his life. The sin he has chosen will warp and twist his life, distort interpersonal relationship, and ultimately bring the dryness of death. But when a follower of the Enemy chooses to do right, he becomes a slave of God, bound to obedience. The believer accepts many limitations the Enemy places on his choices. But in accepting those limitations, the human finds an enriched life, rich relationships, and the present enjoyment of his eternal life—and we are spited.

Let me repeat: any choice a human makes involves slavery. All he can choose is whom he will serve—God or evil. Either choice turns him to a future that is severely limited.

This is a paradox of Enemy ethics. If His followers choose the limitations of obedience to Him, they become truly free. By surrender to the Enemy, humans are lifted to what He calls the "glorious liberty of the children of God."

You see, what humans need is not freedom in their sense at all. We confuse them at this point. We make them believe that release from limitations is a desirable goal. But what every human truly needs is to make choices that will bring him good and not harm, safety and not danger, fulfillment and not emptiness, gain and not loss. What good is "freedom" to a human if the choices he makes destroy him?

Now, it is always the Enemy's strange desire to do good by these grubby animals. The ways of righteousness to which He calls them were fashioned in love. Every "do not" warns against some disaster, while every "do" points to some fresh joy. His narrow pathway, which *appears* restricted, is a magnificent open meadow in which His followers can laugh and play and love and relax and find peace and joy. Those who surrender their "freedom" and choose the slavery of obedience to Him find the fullest meaning of human life. And *that* is freedom indeed.

But, as the Enemy himself admits, it is a narrow way He holds out to them, and "few there be that find it." We on the other hand offer humans the broad vista of a fantasy freedom. We release them to choose any sin their hearts may desire. But with each choice of sin, we guide them deeper into a maze that leads only to destruction. We whisper to them that they are "free" now . . . they have rejected the demands of what God says is "right." They have chosen instead to do whatever they want. When the chains forged by sin drag them by their crushing weight into our ready hands, they will discover that their freedom was a fantasy all along.

I hope, young fiends, that you have seen the practical implications of my discussion. Let me summarize:

1. Keep the gaze of the humans on law as a stone god, until the weight of Law's demand seems to crush them.

2. Many humans will reject both law and the righteousness law expresses. Convince them this reaction is a step toward "freedom."

3. Always link the word *freedom* with the word *from*. Soon rejection of God's moral principles will be confused with liberation. Sinners will be praised for evil, and labeled the "beautiful people" of the present world.

4. Never let a client stop to think that his only real choice is between one set of limitations or another. Humans will always be slaves, either to righteousness or to sin. The great difference is in the wages each pays. Sin offers a fantasy of liberty, and ultimate death. Righteousness holds out life.

5. Remember that the freedom humans truly need is freedom to choose what is to their benefit, and avoid that which harms. So true freedom for humans can only come by following the Enemy in total obedience, for He cares and leads them for their good.

You must always muddy their thinking at this point. Make obedience seem restrictive, and paint disobedience as "freedom." Promise them anything. But be assured that what we will *give* them is what *we* desire . . .

Their pain.

Their misery.

And their loss.

And do be encouraged. The Enemy's way *is* narrow. There are only a few, even among His disciples, who find it. What chance does a still small voice calling men to an unpopular choice have against the flashing lights and neon signs of a whole society calling them to a fantasy freedom that destroys?

LECTURE NINE
Tuesday, 12 February 32913

Authority: The Chains of Command

Imagine a human driving his car along a desert road. He's miles from any city or town, on a perfectly flat plain. Then ahead he sees a traffic signal. As he drives toward it he watches it turn: green, yellow, red; green, yellow, red. When he nears, the light turns red.

There's no car but his on the desert. Yet he slows. He stops. And he waits for the green to tell him to go. Finally the light changes, and he moves on through the intersection.

In this incident we have a picture of law, the stone god. The traffic signal is inflexible, impersonal. It changes on a fixed schedule, unresponsive to the number of cars that may be on the road. It carries with its signal a moral imperative. The driver is restrained only by a sense of "ought." He accepts the notion that violating that external law would somehow be wrong, even though he is alone on the highway.

I tell you this story to contrast the issues raised by the words *law* and *authority*. For authority is something *personal*, not *impersonal*. While law claims to be general or universal, authority is essentially situational.

For instance, follow the driver of that car. As he moves on he comes to a small town, and notices that the highway is blocked. As he pulls up to the blockade, a man dressed as a policeman holds up his hand.

"Sorry, sir, but you'll have to detour. The highway is closed through town."

"Closed! But I don't see anything on the road."

"Sorry, sir. You have to take the road to your right. It'll only add five miles to your trip."

"Five miles! But I have an appointment I have to make."

"The road is closed."

"But *why?*"

"Listen, buddy. I said the road is *closed*. Now move on to that side road or I'll run you in."

Now, *that* is authority. That is a conflict between two persons in a specific situation in which one has the power to make the other do what *he* wants. And if the person under authority does not respond, the person with authority can force compliance.

Actually the word closest to *authority* in the Enemy's handbook—*exousia* in the original language—means "freedom of choice, right, power," and thus "authority." *The one with power has the freedom to choose, not only for himself but for others.* Always with authority, as it is experienced in the present world, there is an implicit conflict of wills. And always implicit is some source of power by which one can force his will on the other. We see it in families:

"Jimmy, time for bed. Nine o'clock."

"Aw, Mom, can't I stay up to watch . . . ?"

"Jimmy! No. Get to bed, *now.*"

We see it in business:

"Charles, I'd like you to stay tonight till this Wilson contract is completed."

"But Mr. Green, I was planning on going to the Little League game. My son is pitching, and it's his first time . . ."

"Charles, I am really sorry, but that contract has *got* to be done tonight. Why not call your son and apologize? I know he'll understand."

"Yes, Mr. Green. I'll do that."

Note the situational nature of each conflict, and note its resolution. Jimmy wants to stay up, but finally he does what Mom chooses for him. Charles wants to go to his son's first Little League game, but he stays and works on the contract. The authority of Mom and Mr. Green were exercised: their wills were imposed on their subordinates.

Human authority rests on the power to punish. This power is not necessarily used, but all know it exists. Mom can punish Jimmy in a variety of ways. She can spank him, withdraw love from him, or even abandon him. Mr. Green can punish Charles by withholding a promotion or raise, transferring him to less significant duty, or even firing him. In human society the notion has taken root that those in authority have the "right" to use their power, and to impose their wills on others. But in the last analysis, authority rests on coercive power to force or command compliance.

The question for us, then, is "How do we use the existence of authority relationships to distort a human's ethical choices?"

To answer, you must first recognize that once sin had entered the world, it was the Enemy Himself who introduced authority—though not as coercive power. You see, before sin there was only one will on earth—the Enemy's. That first pair lived and moved and loved in perfect harmony with that one will. They freely chose what the Enemy had chosen for them.

But with sin came a *multiplication of wills*. Adam and Eve claimed the right to choose their way apart from God's will. Now each human claims to be his own final authority. In this they carry some resemblance to our courageous Father Below, who also determined to stand *beside* the Enemy on the throne of the universe, rather than to stand one step below.

Now, the Enemy recognized the fact that only chaos would exist if each human exercised his will without any limitations. So the Enemy introduced authority—not to control but to provide order. He designed authority structures for all human relationships, from those in the family to those in the business and political realms. The Enemy tells His people to "be subject" to these authorities for *His* sake. He tells them that He is capable of working all things for their good *through* existing authorities, even though in some situations this may seem impossible.

The Enemy views authority relationships as providing order in society—a way to work through conflict between contrary wills in relative harmony. To that end the Enemy gives guidance to those who have authority, and to those under authority. Both need that instruction. For we can warp humans in either position, and pressure them into patterns which fit our ethics of Hell.

How? Ah, it's all so easy, especially when we deal with those who *have* authority. Here are some ways:

1. Make authority an excuse for oppression. Humans are, after all, sinners. So it's not hard for us to suggest that somehow authority is related to inherent superiority, and that it gives a person a right to lord it over others.

We've done some fine work among Christians in this area with the Enemy's notion that "the husband is the head of the wife." Not so much in the grosser situations, like one client family in California where I had the man stalking through the house and literally shouting at his family, "I'm head of this house! I'm the only one here who counts!" No, usually our distortions are more subtle. Whisper to the husband whose wife likes to visit museums that they *ought* to do the backpacking he enjoys because he is the head and "it will be good for her."

When a man's wife has talents and skills, and wants to work, let him feel his manhood and his position of authority threatened. "Not while I'm the head of this house!" he'll finally explode. "It's my job to work and earn our money; it's your job to stay in the house and take care of me and the family."

When it comes to the family, be sure Dad and Mom see "authority" over their kids as an obligation to make all decisions. Carry this over into business; make a boss panic at the thought of a subordinate making any decisions. Carry it into the Church. Require everything, from the color of paint for the basement to the expenditure of all money over ten dollars to be specifically authorized by the Church board.

In each case we make those with authority perceive it as their right and obligation to make all choices for others "under" them. When authority is exercised this way—to rob others of their right to make decisions and thus to reflect God's image in their personhood—then that authority is exercised oppressively. Only good for us will result.

2. Distort the goal of authority. This is especially easy with believers. They can easily be convinced that the purpose of authority is to "break the sinful will" of the person *under* authority—or at least to protect the subordinates from themselves.

That "break the will" notion is delightful to observe in families. You can often convince Christian parents that they are obligated to spank a six-month-old child who cries when Daddy says to be quiet, because it is necessary to "break his sinful will." You can tell them that when a two-year-old says "No!" he should be pounded with a belt or stick.

One great advantage of our "break their will" approach is that it excuses any anger a parent may feel at the child's disobedience. "Parental authority" will be sufficient excuse for brutality, and Mom and Dad will never have to wonder if perhaps sin has distorted their reactions as much as it has distorted the child's actions.

Actually, the Enemy never intended authority to be used for breaking anyone's will. Having will, the capacity to choose, is necessary to being a person. God does not want to rob humans of their wills, any more than He would crush their minds or emotions. No, His goal is to help humans develop their ability to choose what is right. He wants, not broken wills, but wills strong enough to choose His way, even when pressures are great. A parent who uses authority to break a child's will is doing our work, not God's. That human has a muddied meaning for *authority*.

We encourage this same distortion in the Enemy's churches. We stress a "pastoral authority" that is muddied by the notion that the poor "sheep" are certain to go astray unless they have one "shepherd" to make all their decisions for them. Because the "ordinary believer" is fickle, or lacks commitment, we suggest believers need a "man of God" to plan and to choose for them.

In these ways we keep children from growing to maturity, and we keep Christians in spiritual infancy. And all this is done in the good name of an "authority" which the Enemy Himself has introduced!

3. Forge chains of command. This popular concept is very helpful to us. It implies each distortion I've described in this lecture, and it sounds so right! After all, isn't God over all? Hasn't He placed some humans *over* others? Aren't husbands over wives, parents over children, and so on? When the Enemy says "children obey your parents," He Himself seems to authenticate this vertical chain.

Or so *we* want it to seem.

This fallacy is found in a simple fact. The Enemy addresses his injunction to obey to the children. But the promoters of the "chain of command" theory take the instruction as though it were addressed to parents, and make its muddied meaning read, "Parents, force your children to obey." The chain of command implies that, while a person at the top relates directly to God, persons in subordinate relationships relate to the human above them *as if he were God!*

Here we have a strange and magnificent perversion! It leads to wives asking husbands what they should do, as if the husband were the Holy Spirit. We have grown single women who appeal to their fathers or brothers to make decisions for them. And if a woman has no relatives, in some places she's told to go to the elders of the church to ask, "Should I take this job?" or "Should I date that person?" They are not taught to ask for insight or advice. They are told to ask someone else to make the decision *for* them. (Certainly during the childhood years human parents will make many decisions for young children. But wise parents soon begin to help their children make decisions themselves.)

It is here we stress the chain of command to parents, or to husbands, or to others in positions of authority. We make it seem that authority carries an obligation to command in all things. "You are to ask me for permission before doing *anything*," is the ultimate distortion of the exercise of authority as the Enemy sees it.

Of course, we pervert authority from the other side as well. We pressure those *under* authority to rebel, by convincing them that they know better than those over them. We convince teenagers that, since they are sure God is leading them to a particular college, and their parents insist they attend a different college, they must rebel. We never let them imagine that if God *is* leading, He is able to move their parents to change their minds. We never let them learn the power that comes from turning the situation over to Him in prayer.

Also, we whisper that whenever authority is being exercised unjustly disobedience and rebellion are excused. We hide passages like the one in Peter's letter that tells slaves to obey even evil masters as "unto the Lord." Instead we suggest that sins of oppression surely must justify sins of rebellion.

You see, from either side, the connotations of *authority* are a rich sea in which to fish for human souls. And we've made many a catch there to the greater glory of Hell.

Here then we have the muddied meaning of *authority*. To humans that word connotes power, superiority, the right to command, and the obligation to make decisions *for* others. To humans under authority, it connotes injustice, compulsion, and the theft of an individual's right to self-determination. Both those with and without authority are easily manipulated by us through these misunderstandings.

What is the Enemy's meaning for *authority?* Amazingly to us (and to most humans), He sees authority as *an opportunity to serve.* Authority in the family means that a parent is in a position to guide and help a child grow to maturity as a strong person. Authority means that the husband, as "head" of the wife, serves as Christ served the Church, by "giving himself for her." The one with authority has the responsibility of watching—not to control, or break wills, but to support others and guide them in healthy paths. According to Enemy ethics, the context in which authority is to be exercised is not one of power, but of love.

Even we can understand why this is necessary, although we do not understand how such a contemptible thing as "love" can achieve results. You see, coercive power can always force compliance. Charles can be made to stay and finish the contract. But coercive power can never achieve commitment. Charles can never be made by that kind of authority to *want* to stay.

The Enemy has never been willing to settle for compliance. You and I enjoy forcing humans to walk in our paths, and the greater rage they may feel at the compulsion the greater our pleasure. But the Enemy is never pleased when humans walk in lock step, chained by commands to a path they did not choose. Unreasonably, He wants them to want the way He points out to them. In His own dealings with mankind, He does not *force* but *invites* obedience. And His wooing of humans to obedience is done in the most sickening tones of love.

Never let your clients wonder if perhaps any authority they exercise should be modeled on the Enemy's way of exercising His authority. For it is the Enemy's intention that among His followers authority should be patterned on His own way of loving guidance. The one with authority is to win the trust of those "under" him by the demonstration of his love in serving them. And response to authority is to flow as love responds to love, not as fear reacts to power.

Even the Enemy's instructions to those "under" authority reflect this reality. To "obey those who have the rule over you" means literally, "be willing to respond to those who have responsibility as your guides."

But we need not trouble ourselves too much about what the Enemy says, as long as we have muddied the meaning of His words. When parents justify their authoritarian ways on the basis of a supposedly biblical "chain of command," and when pastors support their claim of the right to run a church and its members on the basis of their "God-given authority," we can be sure that the Enemy's meaning has been swallowed up by ours.

So let them look in Scripture for phrases that support their notions. Let them oppress each other with demands for obedience—no matter how wrongly they themselves lead. And don't worry. They will never even hear the words of the Invader, who showed His followers what the Enemy means by authority, and who taught them in these forgettable words:

You know that the rulers of the Gentiles lord it over them, and their high officials exercise authority over them. Not so with you. Instead, whoever wants to become great among you must be your servant, and whoever wants to be first must be your slave—just as the Son of man did not come to be served, but to serve, and to give his life as a ransom for many.

A *servant* as an example of one with authority? Oh no, they'll think. And they'll hurry on to read His words with our meanings, and so become captives to the ethics of Hell.

LECTURE TEN
Thursday, 14 February 32913

Truth: The Outer Limit

Humans these days are extremely skeptical about truth. They're not sure what truth is, or whether it exists. Most think if truth does exist, no one can know it. This gives us a number of significant opportunities to tempt and to deceive.

Of course, philosophers have always raised questions about truth. But the mass of humanity in other ages simply muddled on, knowing intuitively that somehow there must be truth. And the mass has always supposed that truth is also more or less known.

Today it's not just the philosophers who doubt. Skepticism, not religion, is the opiate of the people. Skepticism provides the tottering foundation on which most humans build their lives. You realize this when you hear them comment that everyone must "find his own truth." Or they'll say something is "true for me" but may not be "true for you." With this usage, they completely muddy the meaning of *truth* as the Enemy defines it.

You want to encourage the contemporary view. Let humans make their subjective experience the criterion for what is "true." Then any evil they choose can be linked with this positive term.

You won't need arguments to prove to your clients the commonly accepted notion that truth is subjective and relative. The mass of humans, as I've noted, seldom think about what they believe anyway. "Why, everybody knows *that!*" is the totally compelling reason most humans give for their views. If anyone should question the common wisdom, there are simple arguments you can use to deceive.

For instance, two people are out on a hillside. There's a mild wind blowing. One pulls his sweater closer, and says, "That's a chilly wind." The other takes her sweater off, remarking, "How mild that breeze feels." Now, is the breeze cold or warm?

Obviously, it is warm for her, but cold for him. So one can say it is true that the wind was warm, and at the same time true that the wind was chilly. The "truth" of the statement depends entirely on the experience of the one making it. The truth is subjective.

Now extend this argument to moral areas. Is living together before marriage a good thing? Tune to any radio phone-in program in the United States, and within a week or so you'll hear someone (usually a woman) explain how living together was a good thing for her and her man/husband/boyfriend/fiancé. In the same breath she's almost sure to say, "Of course, this might not be true for everyone." Her moral truth is subjective, not objective.

It's obvious that no one would carry this view of truth to a study of history or into a courtroom. "Napoleon won the Battle of Waterloo" is the kind of statement no subjectivist would try to defend. No one would say in a court of law, "Well, to me there were three shots. Of course, to someone else there might have been one or five."

People today talk in subjective and relativistic ways about morals and ethics and religion *because they have previously rejected the idea that there are objective moral, ethical, and religious truths.* Because they deny truth (except when talking about the kind of facts associated with historical events), they are left with nothing but *opinions* on which to make evaluations. But *opinion* is a weak word. It has no moral connotations. So humans, struggling to maintain a moral appearance, have fallen into calling their opinions "truths."

You see of course why these words *for me* or *for you* have to be added in the modern usage of *truth*. Opinions are always *my* opinions or *your* opinions. There is never an "absolute opinion," as there used to be an "absolute truth." Since opinions are subjective, whenever humans say *truth* and mean *opinion*, they let each other know what they mean by adding "for me" or "for you."

How are contemporary "truths" arrived at? The accepted source is personal experience. "How can I know unless I try it?" is the view of most humans these days. Rather than man being the measure of all things, we have the happy situation in which *each* modern man is the measure of all things *for himself.* Because contemporary man has rejected the idea that there can be absolute truths in areas of religion, morals, and ethics, and has substituted opinion shaped by personal experience, we have a wonderful opportunity. Use that opportunity, and encourage people to "try it for yourself." This basic tenet of modern wisdom sounds quite reasonable to nearly everyone.

The "try it" philosophy is particularly applicable to ethical choices involving the body, or man's sensual nature. Young children sniff glue. Teens taste marijuana and beer. Older teens sample cocaine and pills. And everyone over thirteen wants to play some kind of game with sex. In all these areas, let them hear the warnings of doctors or psychologists or preachers. "Grass lowers motivation," the experts will say. But just whisper to the young teen, "Maybe for some, but maybe not for you. Try it and see if it's true for you." Let young people hear old-fashioned warnings against heavy petting and the problems it creates. Just whisper in their ears: "Maybe for some. But not for you." In almost every case they will try it, to see if it's "true for me."

What is particularly humorous to us is that no one who takes the "try it and see" approach stops to wonder how he'll *know* whether "it's good" or "it's bad" is "true for him." Actually, most people make that decision according to whether or not they like the sensation.

No human ever hears "Ten years of learning math is good for a person's mental processes" and then says, "I'll try it and see." The "try and see" approach to anything implies some immediate gratification. But when someone warns, "Heavy petting will warp your relationships and make it hard to move toward a stable marriage," they will want to try and see. And then they form their opinions not on the basis of long-term results, but on the basis of whether or not they like their present feelings! The only time a person finds out the real impact of such choices is when it's too late!

Moral behavior nearly always has a time lag between action and impact. This is as true for good actions as well as for bad. The young person who says no may lose some short-term popularity. The benefits of that choice may not appear until years and years later. In fact, for some humans ethical choices made in response to the Enemy's truth may provide no apparent benefits until Eternity! So we can easily confuse them about this. We can convince them that whether they like the sensations or not is in fact the test of truth, and is the one reliable measure of whether a particular action is good or bad, right or wrong, "for them."

So far I've spoken about the subjective meaning of *truth* as the moderns use that word—meaning an opinion, verified by personal experience. I've suggested that we encourage this muddied, subjective distortion. But there are other twists to the term we can take advantage of.

I've already noted that *true* and *truth* are positive terms to humans. We take advantage of that residue of implied good when we have our clients use "it's true to life" as justification for publicizing sin. This happens constantly. Does someone raise objections to a scandal-ridden biography? Another is sure to reply, "But it's true, isn't it?" Does a League of Decency object to soap operas, whose plots feature murders, rapes, divorces, adulteries, and every sort of human perversion? Then let the sponsors self-righteously object that it's only "true to life." The very fact that many humans actually live such warped lives seems sufficient evidence that it's appropriate for others to focus their thoughts on such behaviors.

Of course, no one ever thinks of publicizing the happy family down the street, where the dad and mom are. faithful to each other and the kids are growing up secure in their parents' affirmation. That is "true to life" also. But no one really wants to hear about the good in others. Sponsors would never get a large enough share of the audience to justify programs or specials on common goodness. No, it is common badness that attracts an audience. And it is common badness that humans somehow feel they have to justify, and do so by arguing it is "true to life."

The Enemy, of course, operates on the opposite tack. He says, "Whatever is true, whatever is noble, whatever is right, whatever is pure, whatever is lovely, whatever is admirable—if anything is excellent or praiseworthy—think about such things." In His system *truth* is intimately related to nobility, righteousness, purity, loveliness—to the admirable, the excellent, and the praiseworthy. It is one of our great victories that in ordinary human speech we have turned this around. Today they associate the true with that which is ignoble, unrighteous, impure, ugly, disgusting, inferior, and deserving of condemnation. It is *our* truth that humans have accepted as reality. It is all those things associated with our truth that their novels, movies, and television programs publicize. It is our truth, the reality of filth, which we use to clog their minds and then label with the Enemy's own term!

To the ordinary twentieth-century human, *truth* in an absolute moral sense does not exist. In its place he has substituted "true for me" or "true to life." The one truth is subjective opinion, the other publicized sin. And both are disguised by having the term *truth* applied to them!

Now, while we have been reshaping the thinking of ordinary persons, we have also been at work with the committed believer. We have primed believers for a reaction to their culture. We have encouraged them to defend truth as an absolute—out there. Thus what they call "God's truth" becomes something splendid and glorious, a system of beliefs that must be defended and taught and argued and defined, but not—and I repeat, *not*—lived.

I remember a letter in which a serious young follower took an author to task for the way he treated "the Kingdom of God" in a book. In some fifteen typewritten pages, the young man exposed error, crushing and smashing it in the dust. And then he commented to the author that he engaged in this "dialogue" not to be critical but because he felt that only by working together to get at truth could Christians find a basis for fellowship in their divided church.

How wonderful for us! This young man never realized that agreement on truth was never meant by the Enemy to provide a basis of fellowship for His followers. (Their relationship to God through the Invader is His basis for their fellowship.) The young man never even realized that he used the word *truth* in a nonbiblical sense. To this human, as to so many who are theologically oriented, *truth* means *a consistent and accurate system of beliefs.* (Usually it means *my* system of beliefs.) The young theologian held (accurately) that there *is* objective truth, and held (inaccurately) that *knowing truth* means squeezing that objective truth into a human theological system.

This idea of truth is extremely gratifying to us. It means on the one hand that generations of Christians battle each other over their ways of talking about the Enemy, and see their feuds as holy wars for truth. It means that in their zeal for truth they forget all about love, and make creedal agreement a requirement for fellowship with each other rather than accepting all children of their Father as brothers and sisters. If we can keep the Enemy's followers fighting over Truth, we keep them divided. And we keep them from grasping the real meaning of truth.

The Invader Himself said it: "You shall know the truth, and the truth shall make you free." Many Christians can quote this verse, but most have no idea what goes before it, and so suppose that theological accuracy is what promises freedom. What the Invader actually said was, "If you keep my teaching, you are really my disciples. Then you will know the truth, and the truth will make you free." It is in *keeping the Enemy's words* that His followers discover the truth, and, in the Enemy's sense of that term, find freedom.

You see, in the Old and New Testaments of the Enemy's book the words for *truth* imply "correspondence with reality." The Enemy, who shaped mankind and this universe, designed into His creation natural moral laws as well as natural physical laws. He alone knows these moral realities, and so He alone can tell humankind the impact of certain moral choices before those choices are made. If one knows ahead of time what will result, one does not have to "try it myself" to find out!

A statement like "fire burns" presents an Absolute, in that whenever a human puts his hand in a fire, he can expect that hand to be burned. No rational human who is told that "fire burns" is going to thrust his hand in the next fire he notices to find out if burning is "true for me."

To talk of moral truth, then, is simply to say that there are laws or principles built into moral creation that are like those in nature. Such things are true not because "God says them." They are true because they accurately portray reality as the Enemy shaped it.

Now, these truths, or realities about the way the Enemy's creation works, were not revealed by Him so that men could construct theological systems, or argue this or that interpretation. His words were spoken so that His followers might order their lives by His revelation. The Enemy's truth, to be known, must be *lived*. And so the Invader says, "if you keep my words, you will know the truth." The kind of truth that God has revealed, as far as ethics and morals are concerned, is *a kind of truth that must be experienced in obedience in order to be known.* The theologian can argue, and the zealot can fight for his interpretation. And both serve *us*, if their emphasis is anything less than encouraging His followers to *live* what they are learning.

So you see how well we have twisted things. We have convinced most humans they must try sin to see if God's warnings against sin are true. And we have convinced many of His followers to insist that others agree with their *interpretation* of truth, whether or not they experience it.

We have made *truth* a suspect word to the modern pagan, and have made *experience* a suspect notion to the modern believer. For each we have muddied the meaning the Enemy gives to truth, and by the confusion have led many—unbelievers and believers alike—into the lifestyle of Hell.

What must we guard against to preserve our great victory here? Very simply this. We must guard against simple believers, who accept the archaic notion that the Enemy has shared a trustworthy portrait of moral and spiritual reality and who therefore commit themselves to experiencing that reality by obeying His words. Such simple-minded individuals would never think of "proving" His words *by* their experience—as though their experience gave His truth its validity. But such simpletons would expect His words to prove themselves *in* their experience. So they would plod forward in their obedient walk with the Enemy. They would listen to His voice, not their own sensations, and whatever the immediate result of obedience, would trust Him enough to believe that His truth will prove trustworthy in the end.

Fortunately for us, this is a soft and selfish age. The Enemy's kind of truth holds few attractions for a generation that has sold itself to immediate sensation, and hesitates to challenge the popular conviction that all truth is relative. So even Christians are likely to speak about their faith apologetically, and mumble something about God's way being best . . . "for me."

"Of course," some will even add, "it may not be best for you."

And so with the abandonment of truth, modern humans (including many of the Enemy's own) have presented themselves to us.

Ah yes.

They have willingly placed themselves in our (shall we say, tender?) hands.

LECTURE ELEVEN
Tuesday, 19 February 32913

Guilt: The Lost Connection

When you deal with humans, you must always remember that they are at heart "moral" beings.

This is easy for us to forget. And they constantly *try* to forget it. As we read their newspapers, observe their private (and, these days, public) lives, the conviction steals over us that humans are essentially immoral. Why, no one could observe their politicians long without arriving at the conclusion that most are either fools or knaves. They seem so eager to trade away the best interests of their nation for votes or money.

As I say, it's all too easy to forget they are moral beings. In spite of all the evidence to the contrary, they are not, as one African tribesman described his people's sexual practices, "like goats."

The thing we must remember is this. Their moral nature is not expressed in what they do, but in what they believe in spite of themselves. The troublemaker Paul analyzed it this way: "When Gentiles, who do not have the law, do by nature things required by the law, they are a law for themselves, even though they do not have the law, since they show that the requirements of the law are written on their hearts, their consciences also bearing witness, and their thoughts now accusing, now even defending them." This is important for us demons to understand . . . and to take advantage of.

Law, as an expression of the Enemy's moral character, is revealed in two ways. The first is in His own writings. The second is in human nature. The creatures do reflect, no matter how imperfectly, His nature. The written law says, "There is right and wrong . . . and this is it." The law planted in human nature says, "There is right and wrong . . . and these are the moral issues." All cultures have moral notions about killing, for example. All say it is wrong to simply kill whomever you like. Some specify who you *can* kill, and when; in the western United States, for instance, it was once considered totally moral to string up a farmer or cowboy who stole another man's horse. The particulars might not agree with the Enemy's written law, but the issues considered *moral issues* are everywhere the same.

It's the same with sex. In no human society has it ever been viewed as "right" to simply take any person one wanted at any time. Cultures differ about how many wives a man may have. But no culture exists without *some* sexual rules.

We can say the same thing about private property, and every other issue covered in the Enemy's ten rules.

Humans, then, express their essential moral nature by establishing standards of right and wrong. The standards may differ in detail from the standards of the Enemy's revelation. But nearly everyone in a society will agree that the rules of that society are morally "right," and that breaking the rules is morally "wrong."

This is what I mean when I say that humans are at heart moral beings. They have an innate awareness of right and wrong as existing in their universe. They agree on the kinds of things that are moral issues. And they feel compelled to establish moral rules or guidelines.

Of course they don't *practice* their moral notions. When the Enemy says, "there is none righteous, no not one," He is making an obvious statement. A society sets up its rules. And everyone in that society proceeds, to a greater or lesser degree, to break them. As the Enemy says, this is because humans are sinners. Their inner being is twisted and misshapen almost as delightfully as ours, though few can compare with one of us in our dark beauty.

All this leaves humans in a strange dilemma. They acknowledge a right and wrong to which their very natures testify. At the same time, they scurry about choosing what they know is wrong.

It is because both these elements exist in humans that there is such a thing as guilt. There is no guilt for goats. They mount one another as the urge arises, and are never troubled afterward. No rules governing right and wrong are recognized by them, so their practices never trouble them. But humans are not like goats. They know there *are* rules. They know it when their behavior violates the rules. Awareness of the gulf between belief and behavior brings with it awareness of a guilt that does not exist for goats.

How does mankind deal with the gulf? How do they react to awareness of guilt? Paul says rightly that they set their minds to accusing and to defending. The human conscience testifies to guilt; the human mind struggles to find ways to deal with guilt.

It is at this point that *we* enter and muddy their thinking. It is at this point that we take a key ethical term, gently disconnect it from its true meaning, and hang all sorts of connotations from it, all of which keep humans from finding the way out of their dilemma! The term that once was the Enemy's, but now serves our purposes, is *guilt*.

The true meaning of *guilt* is quite simple. The ancient word most commonly translated "guilt" meant origin, or cause. It was usually used in a negative sense, as accusation or blame, indicating responsibility attached to an act. Inevitably the early usage associated responsibility for an act with its consequences.

Thus in the Enemy's handbook guilt, sin, and punishment are all bound up together. We can summarize the Enemy's meaning for *guilt* by defining it as "the responsibility of a man for his actions, together with the resultant consequences." At heart the word *guilt* expresses the recognition by humans of three things:

I have done wrong.

I am responsible for my wrong acts.

I deserve to bear the consequences (be punished).

Because humans *are* moral beings, each of these aspects of guilt is evident to them. Charged by their own consciences, men and women turn their thoughts to accuse or excuse themselves.

A human's conscience shouts out its condemning charge, "You've sinned!" The human, being a moral person, recognizes in spite of himself that he deserves punishment. But he is wisely terrified of the thought that *God* might punish him. So, to avoid facing the reality of God's judgment, the human often *accuses himself*. He wallows in self-condemnation and feelings of guilt. Unconsciously he hopes that this self-inflicted punishment will be penalty enough. Perhaps the ultimate Judge will accept self-torment as sufficient retribution.

Of course, he does not consciously think this all out. The word *God* may never even flit across his thoughts. He might not even be aware that he *is* punishing himself! It is simply that as a moral being, a human knows intuitively that sin/responsibility/punishment *are* connected. And so he punishes himself—to assuage his guilt or perhaps to avoid the greater consequences of his actions.

Other humans, when their consciences shout, "you've sinned!"

attempt excuses. "You'd have done the same if you were in my situation," they whine. Or with outrage they cite the great disadvantages of their childhoods; the fact that Mom and Dad divorced is the real cause of their actions!

Both accusing and excusing approaches have their merits. But they also have their dangers. Let a person condemn himself too much, and he may become miserable enough to seek out the Enemy for relief. Let a person make too obvious an excuse, and he may not be able to hide from himself the fact that, whatever pressures he experienced, he was still responsible for his choices.

So we have come up with a better way. Our better way is to sever the connections between the word *guilt* and its original meaning! With the connection between guilt and responsibility, or guilt and acts of sin, or guilt and punishment broken, we gain a distinct advantage over the Enemy and, of course, over the pulpy slugs that we deceive.

Let's look at each connection, and see how we have shattered it.

1. *The connection between guilt and acts of sin.* Our staff in the Department of Dissimulation has already succeeded in this task. In modern culture the word *guilt* is universally taken to mean "guilt feelings." Humans are deeply concerned about their guilt feelings. They rush to psychiatrists to get rid of them. They get angry at themselves for feeling guilty. Or they get depressed because they can't shake the nagging feeling that something is wrong.

Of course, such feelings are not always identified by humans as "guilt feelings." But when they do identify them, it is to our great advantage that these clods focus on the feelings and not on any of the acts of sin that are the sources of true guilt. Keep humans confused on this. Guilt itself is not a feeling. Guilt is a fact, linked specifically with an act. Because a human did sin, and is responsible, he is under the burden of just consequences. God, who is a moral judge, will punish. But if we can keep humans thinking of guilt as a feeling, they will try to deal with the feeling and not the sin! And they will be truly lost.

Helping them to redefine acts of sin is another way. We separate guilt and acts of sin. We have them call their adulteries "love affairs." We name fits of anger "righteous indignation." We encourage them to smirk when they hear of a person cheating on his income tax, and call it clever. We have them demand "rights" for homosexuals to imply the rightness of their "alternative lifestyle." We move them to label their prevarications "white lies." They will be eager to do all this. It seems much more attractive to them than to face up to actions as sins, that is, willful violations of the commandments of God and their own consciences.

2. *The connection between guilt and responsibility.* This battle too has, to all intents and purposes, been won by us already.

Human systems of justice make excuses for murderers and rapists. Juries are swayed by appeals to the disadvantaged backgrounds of the criminal.

More close to home, humans tend to blame their guilt feelings not on personally responsible acts, but on "puritan ethics" or "Victorian values." Such outmoded ways of thinking, the reasoning goes, have made people *feel* guilt about performance of normal and natural actions! Mom and Dad get their share of the blame too. They "imposed" values. The present generation has intellectually rejected the old values, so the argument goes, but the hang-ups of the past generation cause completely unjustified feelings of guilt.

In these ways humans try to make others responsible either for their actions or for the feelings that follow their choices. The fact is that, because he is a moral being, doing wrong makes a person aware of guilt. Humans are conscious of the moral gap between what they acknowledge to be right and the choices they make. They blame others for "making" them too weak to choose right. They blame others for the nagging awareness of standards which they tell themselves over and over again are not real. In both these ways we help them deny responsibility for their actions and for themselves.

3. *The connection between guilt and punishment.* This too is something we encourage humans to deny. We suggest they dismiss the Enemy as an old-fashioned notion. Or we help them reshape Him into a benevolent, doddering fool who is so pleased when a human bothers to think of Him He would never hold any sins against him.

If a human is a believer, we stress the love of God to the extent that His holiness and righteousness and justice are stripped away. We disguise love as a soft, squishy sweetness, like that of a mother who never denies her children sweets and goodies, who watches them grow fatter and more unhealthy week by week, but who passes over her indulgence by labeling it "love." That weak and cowardly kind of love is just the kind of love we want them to imagine when they speak of God.

We want to engage humans in campaigns to release murders from the death sentence. Be sure in such campaigns to build sympathy for the murderers and to never mention the persons the killers robbed of life. Talk about it being wrong for the state to kill, as though the death sentence were a fiat act by government with no connection at all to the murderous actions of the condemned.

We want humans to begin early to disassociate guilt and punishment. No matter what a child does, tell his parents he must never be spanked. As he gets older, and breaks a neighbor's window, have Mom and Dad pay for it themselves rather than having the child face the homeowner and work off his debt. When the youth is older still, be sure the parents continue to bail him out of the consequences of his misdeeds. He'll grow up learning the lesson *we* want to teach: that there are no consequences to evil acts.

When the connection between guilt and acts of sin, guilt and personal responsibility, and guilt and consequences is lost, the whole concept of guilt as it is portrayed in the Enemy's handbook is sucked dry of meaning. Then guilt, which the Enemy meant to turn men to Him, no longer confronts humans; it no longer shouts of a danger from which only God can save.

But suppose you cannot muddy the meaning of guilt to the necessary degree. Suppose some human still recognizes his responsibility for his own acts of sin, and realizes the resultant consequences? All is not yet lost. Then we must use guilt to repel from God rather than to draw men to Him.

We do this by making God seem vast, impersonal, and judgmental—the great stone god of law turned angry. In the face of that vision of retribution which most will quickly imagine, the normal man turns to flee. As with Adam and Eve at the time of their first sin, we take the humans by the hand and guide them deeper into the forest, fanning their vain hope that they can elude God.

Always, when they feel guilt, encourage them to flee! Stir up terror! Never let them, when they have recognized guilt, think of how a loving human father would relate to his erring child. Never let them visualize the child, tear-stained, coming to Daddy to confess. Never let them visualize after the spanking the sobs of relief and hugs of reconciliation. Never give them even the most shadowy glimpse of the fact that God names Himself Father in His handbook. Never let them stop to realize that He, who is all good, can hardly be less eager for reconciliation than a human father who is at best only partly good.

And never, never let them see that in the Invasion of the Enemy's Son, and in His death, the flogging they deserve was given, and received, by God. Never let them look at Calvary, to discover there the Eternal consequences of each man's sins. Never let them hear the proclamation, "Paid in Full," or see it written on the cross in blood.

Our hope is that guilt will bring such shame and fear that it must be hidden or denied. Our hope is that guilt will bring such suppressed terror that humans will clutch in panic at the escape *we* offer, and break the connections of guilt with reality. If they once realize that guilt, in the context of God's love for man, need not terrify but can be dealt with openly because God has dealt with it already . . . well, then it is we who will have lost.

And it is they who, by facing guilt for what it is and God for who He is, will have won.

LECTURE TWELVE
Thursday, 21 February 32913

Forgiveness: The Extinction of Pride

In one sense, today's subject does not belong in a study of the ethics of Hell. We know of no such thing as "forgiveness" in our relationships with each other, or with our human clients. Our delight is to snare them in the webs of sin. We watch them wander on, unaware at first that they're entangled. We smother a laugh as they finally begin to struggle. We shout with joy when their panic grows. And finally we feast on their terror when they are wrapped so tightly they cannot move at all.

But how we shudder when the Enemy steps in. With a stroke of forgiveness He can sever the strands sin has woven and set them free. How we rage when He delivers them from the consequences of a hellishly immoral life, and takes them to Himself *anyway!*

But like it or not, "forgiveness" must be included in these lectures. Not so much because we can twist the word to lead humans away from moral action. No, instead we twist the word to defend ourselves and our victims against that lightning raid by the Enemy. We must twist it well, and cloud its meaning, to keep Him from snatching more humans from our hands.

Once again, humans are our greatest allies. They have already muddied the word *forgiveness* with strange meanings that mask the reality it signifies. Let's look at these distortions.

1. Forgiveness is weakness. One of my favorite poems, written by a human now twisting in a despair that mocks his words, goes something like this:

I am the master of my fate:
I am the captain of my soul.

There's something, one might say, "manly" about those words. "I have chosen for myself!" the poet seems to say. "Whatever happens, I accept responsibility for my choices, and I am man enough to bear the consequences." My favorite song, by the way, is one a human crooner of some accomplishment made famous: "I did it my way."

Ah, how attractive that sounds to humans.

We can see it even in two-year-olds. "Let me help you into the car, Jimmy." "No! I do it myself!" So Mom stands back to watch young Jimmy struggle up onto the seat beside her. Even if Mommy is in a hurry, and annoyed at Jimmy's slow efforts, there's still a tinge of pride as she watches her little big boy do for himself.

Foster that spirit of self-reliance. After a series of bad choices when everything falls apart, encourage humans to take a perverse pride in taking the consequences "like a man."

"I made the mistake," you can easily get a human to say, "and I'm man enough to pay the penalty." Lead your human client to think there is something heroic about going down with his ship like the captains of old days, even when there's a lifeboat standing by and others eager to throw him a line.

As the cold waters cover his head and his lungs strangle for air, he'll have the satisfaction of going down "like a man" . . . and we'll have the satisfaction of mocking his pride as he is crushed to screaming terror at the reality of Hell.

2. Forgiveness is license. This is an attractive distortion to the very moral. They often feel that the only motive for doing right is fear or a sense of obligation.

"Why," they will say, "if you can be *forgiven* so easily, what's to keep a person from going out and doing anything he pleases?"

In their minds, a proclamation of forgiveness would simply tear down the bars that restrain the animal in man. Everyone would rush headlong out to sin. Even moral humans would be unable to hold down the dark impulses that rage in their imaginations . . . or so they think.

Actually, of course, some humans *do* distort forgiveness into license. But these are the ones already looking for an excuse to do what they want. The argument that forgiveness is a license to sin seems strongest to those who are looking for chains to keep them from doing what they do *not* want to do. Because they are moral, they feel a deep obligation to do right, and the temptations to sin that surge now and then bother them deeply. They feel that only the terror of judgment holds them back. If these restraints were removed, they do not know what they might do, and so are afraid.

How laughable this is to us. How rich a joke, that these humans fear forgiveness when it is actually one of the Enemy's most

powerful weapons *against* sin. But keep them fearing. Keep them
in terror. Cast images of all sorts of attractive sins in their minds.
Let them feel the pull of temptation, and then whisper that only
fear of punishment keeps them from surrendering to evil. In that
state of mind, any message of forgiveness will not only be
unheard, but will be fought against frantically!

3. Forgiveness is deserved. This is a way to cheapen forgiveness, and make it meaningless. For many, forgiveness is an "of
course" kind of thing, and demanded as a right!

"A little thing like sleeping with my boyfriend? Why, we're
both consenting adults. Of course I'm forgiven . . . if there's
anything to forgive."

For many in this modern age there is *nothing* that doesn't
deserve forgiveness. A driver goes through a red light and rams a
car, killing a young woman. "But he was drunk, and didn't know
what he was doing. He was terribly sorry afterward." Ah well.
Even the courts say, "Put him on probation."

"My son broke into a house and stole a television set? But he's
just a kid! It was only a prank. Certainly you're not going to
charge him. Why, that would go on his record!"

Even murder these days is taken so lightly that some feel a
killer should be treated gently and given a short jail sentence
rather than execution.

In all these illustrations, we see a trend that we have worked
hard to support coming to fulfillment in modern society. We have
gradually drained sin of its *wrongness*. Driving while drunk, and
endangering innocent people, does not seem wrong enough to
merit punishment. Vandalizing a school, or breaking into a house
to steal, doesn't seem wrong enough to deserve a blot on a
youth's record. No wonder that in such a society even killing
another human does not seem wrong enough to demand the
appropriate penalty. A "life sentence" (with parole in seven
years) will do.

In this kind of society, personal sins also can be lightly excused
as minor things, not deserving God's concern and *therefore*
forgiveable. When we cheapen sin as we have so effectively, we
cheapen forgiveness, and drain it of its meaning as well.

4. Forgiveness demands being sorry. This is another of our
finer ploys. If a human will not fall into the trap of thinking his
sins are insignificant, then let us make him think that they are
terrible. Remind him over and over again that he does not
deserve forgiveness. Convince him that only if he *truly* repents,

and is deeply sorry for his failures, might the Enemy possibly consider his petitions for forgiveness.

Once we get a human thinking along these lines, we have him! Now in his mind forgiveness is based on *his* action, not on the Enemy's. And he will always fall short of performing whatever works he feels are necessary to merit being forgiven.

In this we have, of course, fastened on *repentance* and twisted its meaning. We have made the word mean "being sorry" to most humans. Thus we've connected repentance with a *feeling,* and if there is one thing humans cannot control it is their feelings. That's why you always want to link the word *truly* with the word *sorry* in your client's thinking.

A client may be feeling totally ashamed and sorry about yelling at his children. He may feel so badly that when one of his children bursts into the room where he is sitting, he shouts even more angrily at being disturbed in his remorse! When the stricken child ducks out of the room, your client will then go back and condemn himself more roundly. If he had been *truly* sorry, he'd tell himself, he would never have shouted the second time! And so the human is drawn even deeper into endless self-examination, trying to make himself feel sorry enough to merit forgiveness. Each time he fails, he will flail himself for his lack of true repentance and sorrow.

All of this self-examination keeps him from discovering what repentance actually means. And keeps him from realizing that forgiveness comes by an act of the Enemy, not by a work of the sinner.

Let me say once again, class, that it is important for us to keep the meaning of forgiveness a secret from humans. Convince them that it is heroic to accept punishment and reject rescue. Terrify them with the notion that forgiveness will act as a license to sin. Drain sin of its wrongness, so forgiveness will seem a cheap and merited response to any evil. If these fail, whisper to the human whose conscience convicts him that he must earn forgiveness by being sorry enough to commend himself to God. And then plague him with doubts that he is "truly" repentant. Thus you will keep humans tangled in our webs. And will ensure their continued exercise of our kind of an ethical life.

But why is it so important to keep humans blind to the meaning of forgiveness? Because forgiveness is not simply remission of the penalty of sin. The Enemy's handbook says that when humans confess their sins, "He is faithful and just to forgive us our sins, and *keep on cleansing us from all unrighteousness."* Forgiveness opens the door to the cleansing, purifying action of God in human lives. As they are purified and made holy by Him, they desert our ethics, and in spite of our utmost efforts begin to live truly righteous lives.

You can see why we need to understand forgiveness. We must keep its true meaning from our clients! At the least hint that a client is gaining insight into the reality *forgiveness* describes, we must frantically bend every effort to distract the brute's attention. Or we must flood his mind with one of the distorted images I've described in this class. But let's go on, and see what it is that we are to be on guard against.

Let's begin by restating something discussed in my last lecture on guilt. In the Enemy's way of thinking, *guilt* relates to responsible acts of sin and their necessary consequences. When a human recognizes his guilt he admits, "I have done wrong. I am responsible for my wrong acts. I deserve to bear the consequences [be punished]."

The Enemy has been very clear on the consequences. "The wages of sin is death," He has said. And "the soul [person] that sins shall die." To the Enemy sin is a terrible thing. Sin can never be dismissed lightly, but for the sake of rightness in the universe must be appropriately punished.

This created a great dilemma for the Enemy. How could He uphold rightness in His universe, and still love mankind? How could He lift up humans to Himself if they are stained with guilt?

The Enemy's solution is completely impossible. We demons each realize there is only one truly significant being in the universe—myself. In the last analysis, class, the only being I care about is me. While I desire your success in your mission of tempting and deceiving, I desire that success for *my* glory. (And for the humiliation of old Glubnose, that idiot you must bear with as dean of this institution of lower learning.)

Certainly our basic selfishness is admirable and completely right. What I do I do for *me,* not for you. Only I have true significance to me, and you are at best *things* for me to use. Just as humans are *things* to us, and never "persons" as they are to the Enemy.

As I said, the Enemy's solution to His dilemma is impossible for us to understand, because it involved His *self-sacrifice.* He, whom even we are forced to recognize as the greatest above all creation, actually stripped Himself of His prerogatives as God.

He crawled around with humans in the dust of their tiny planet, and then allowed Himself to be nailed like a common criminal to a cross. He bore the physical pain. He accepted the spiritual anguish, knowing in an instant/Eternity the ultimate consequences of sin. He experienced the anguish of separation from His Father and source of Life.

And then, shattering our one time of great rejoicing, He threw dust in our faces by rising to life again. Risen, He announced to all humankind the forgiveness of sins through the merits of His blood!

He took the punishment for sin that guilt demands. With the debt fully paid, He is now free to offer all men forgiveness. And that forgiveness which is held out in Him and by Him comes with the gift of a new and righteous life.

Some of His followers have rightly described divine forgiveness as an *exchange of life.* He takes their sin, and gives them His own righteousness. Daily he takes their failure and weakness and charges it off against the credit of His cross. Daily He gives them new strength and power to walk the pathway of their life in His righteousness.

And what does He ask from them?

Nothing!

Simply admission of their need, with trust in Him as the forgiving God, and the transaction's done. Unselfishly, because of something He calls *love,* He *gives* without charge that which they could never earn.

When a human comes to understand forgiveness, we cannot even gain a daily advantage! We cannot even twist repentance to mean sorrow. For the human discovers that all God expects of him is to acknowledge sin as sin, and trust God to cleanse and transform him.

How humiliating.

How shameful for us, who work so hard to turn a human down our paths, to then hear through his mind an inner voice command "About face!" How humiliating to see that human change his mind about his sin, turn around, and with strength provided by assured forgiveness march back to the Enemy's narrow way. This is perhaps the bitterest time we have to face. Until, of course . . . well never mind. That time is a long way off. For now, selfishness rules in our dark kingdom. And *we* rule the world of men.

LECTURE THIRTEEN

Tuesday, 26 February 32913

Love: A Maze of Love

I am devoting two lectures to the topic of love, partly because love is at the heart of Enemy ethics, and partly because love is so powerful a word in *our* ethics as well. Rightly twisted, love is like every other ethical concept of the Enemy's. It can be used to lead those pulpy human creatures through our maze of sin.

The concept of love has always been a complex maze. The Greeks, who shaped the language the Enemy used for His so-called "New Testament," had several words for love and a variety of meanings. *Phileo,* for instance, meant "to regard with affection." It was used mainly for the attraction of people to each other, for close relationships such as in the family. That word brings images of concern, of caring, of hospitality.

Another word, *eros,* reflects the relationship between men and women. It has a tone of longing, of craving, of desire. This kind of love is often viewed as a dominating passion, moving humans to rush toward ruin, forgetting all reason and discretion in search of ecstasy. This is a meaning of love which brings us great ethical advantage.

A final word is *agape.* In secular Greek this was a pale word, a colorless synonym for fondness. It was this almost neutral word that the Enemy infused with new strength and power. It is this word that is at the root of Enemy ethics, as we shall see next lecture.

Today, however, the humans use a single word, *love,* to cover all these ideas. The word itself is ethically positive, and powerful. Say *love* and unless a human is in heat, or reading one of our slick pornographic products, humans will think of a child reaching up for a father's hand. They will have the warm impression of a neighbor welcoming a friend into his home. Or they will feel the rightness of tenderness and loyalty in a marriage that grows fonder over the years.

These impressions are wonderful for us. Even when love is totally selfish and devouring, the word *love* is so linked with good that it disguises the evil. What a beautiful thing *that* is! How glorious that humans, in their muddled way, tend not to make distinctions between selfless love and selfish love, even when they use the word to talk about ethics and morals!

For instance, one of the most powerful of modern ethical notions is "love makes it right." We often use this to encourage sex sins. Formerly the excuse, "But we really love each other" was something only young people used. Now the older generation uses it as well! Several things are interesting about this reasoning. First, what kind of "love" do the humans who say it mean?

There is a disgusting cluster of the Enemy's followers called the Order of the Manse. They run Brother Juniper restaurants in many cities to support themselves and their ministries. Their whole purpose in life is to serve, and they give unstinting love to life's castaways. Their love is a sickening reflection of the Enemy's, an unselfish spending of themselves to benefit others who cannot repay them in kind.

Now, notice what is really being said by a couple who justify sexual involvement by saying, "We love each other." They are not talking about the kind of love that faithfully spends itself to serve. They are talking about love as an attraction each feels for the other. They may even be talking about passion, and the powerful desire aroused by each other's sensuality. The "We love" uttered by members of the Order of the Manse means, "I give." The "We love" uttered by the coupling pair means, "We each receive!"

How foolish the phrase, "but we love each other" is when given as justification for *any* behavior. What a human *may* be saying is, "I care enough to give myself to gain the best interests of another." But a human *may* be saying instead, "I care about the thrills and sensations *I* get from her." Until humans define the kind of "love" they mean, the words "I love you" or "We love each other" are ethically meaningless.

There are in fact ways to be sure of the kind of "love" truly in view. If a human says "I love you" in the dark, in the back seat of a car, instead of saying it in public in front of friends and relatives at a wedding, then even the greatest fool should suspect that what is meant is, "I crave sex and want it from you." Or when humans use "we love each other" to excuse *any* behavior, anyone should know they mean selfish love. After all, no one needs an *excuse* for something he doesn't already feel is wrong! So if anyone gives "but I love" *as an excuse,* he is saying that he involved the partner in something wrong! Self-sacrificing love never entices others to do wrong. Self-sacrificing love protects and cares for others enough to surrender momentary personal pleasures for the others' benefit.

How we stand back in amazement and watch these creatures deceive themselves! How delighted we are when they believe their own excuses, and convince themselves that self-love, involving the use of another human as an object for their pleasures, makes a wrong right! How amazing that they can use "love" in such an obviously selfish way, and not even recognize their own or their partner's basic selfishness.

We certainly want humans to use the phrase "we love each other" to justify all sorts of selfish behavior. We want them to use these words to cover sin with a façade of righteousness.

Now, our ethics does insist that "love makes it right." To us love *is* self-love. Our own selfish advantage is true morality here in Hell.

It won't do, however, to have humans think about these things. It will never do to let them get straight the simple fact that in Enemy ethics, any "love" that is invoked to justify any sin is necessarily selfish. So encourage humans to use the words "We love each other" to justify all sorts of selfish behavior, and they need never realize that selfish love never makes *anything* right.

Part of the complexity of the term *love* can be found in the fact that often selfish love can't be recognized. Many acts that humans describe as good or benevolent or right may be motivated by selfish love. A human makes a generous contribution to a charity . . . and is shown in a news photo smiling modestly as he presents the check. Or a human makes a quiet contribution to an orphanage and feels a little less guilty about the way he gained his money. Even members of a church, making up their annual Thanksgiving baskets for the poor, may have less than pure motives for their "charity."

My point is a simple one. "Good" actions, while they appear to be loving, may not in fact have love as their motivation. Most acts by humans are based on another principle entirely.

That principle has been called the "norm of reciprocity." In simple terms: "You scratch my back, I'll scratch yours." You see, humans operate sort of a social barter system with each other. One invites another over for dinner. And expects to be invited back in return. They send Christmas cards to their friends. If a friend does not send them a card, next year they scratch him off the list.

The Invader, when He was here on earth, spoke about such trade-offs. Here are His words about reciprocity-love:

> If you love those who love you, what reward will you get? Are not even the tax collectors doing this? And if you greet only your brothers, what are you doing more than others? Do not even pagans do that?

What He was saying is quite clear. Love, as fondness or attraction, can be developed between friends by doing good to one another. A love for those who love or do good to you is known and experienced by everyone, no matter how evil in other ways. Who hasn't heard the excuse given for some brutal killer, "But he really loves dogs and children!"

The Invader points out, and we agree, that such "love" gains no great moral credit, because it's a love that is repaid. This love also is selfish, to the extent that it pays benefits. It is selfish to the extent that when the benefits are removed (the other couple does not return our dinner invitation, or a spouse does not respond to affection) this kind of "love" withers.

But suppose a human realizes that "love" used as an excuse for sin must be selfish. Suppose he realizes that much "love" humans experience is ethically neutral, and actually describes the principle of reciprocity. We still have a way to confuse them. We teach them that *selfless love . . . is enough.*

This notion makes motive alone the sole criterion for ethical choices. For instance, let's say that an individual *truly* has a friend. He has only ten dollars and the friend has nothing. But the friend needs money to get a bus ticket to visit a sick parent. Desiring the best for the friend, the first individual gives him the ten dollars, even though he now has no money. Clearly this is selfless love, in that it considers what is good for the friend, and acts on that basis even at personal cost.

This is a clear-cut case. But let's look at a more complicated one. Let's suppose the friend is a student, who has to take an examination. But the friend has been ill, and unable to prepare for the test. It's vital he pass the test, to get out of school in time to get an important job. So he asks for help. Should a person cheat, and give him the answers to the test questions?

The first person now must make a choice. He does not believe cheating is right, normally. But this is a special case, and surely cheating seems in the best interests of his friend who must pass the examination. Doesn't love demand that he do what is best for his friend? In spite of the fact that helping his friend involves cheating?

Those who insist love alone is a sufficient guide to ethical action would tend to cheat as "the loving thing to do" and thus as a moral and right action. In essence, they argue that *intention* determines the morality of human choices. If the intention is good, and the motive one of concern for another's highest good, then any action is truly moral and thus right.

Now, we know this is nonsense. It's as reasonable to say that a person who starts a fire in the stairwell of an old apartment house to light the way upstairs for a child has chosen what is right. Even if the fire does not spread and burn down the apartment building, *the intention of the person lighting the fire did not make his action praiseworthy!* The means he chose to carry out his intention was so foolish that the action harmed others rather than helped. His motive was good but the means was bad.

Now apply this to ethics. The motive of helping a friend pass a test may be praiseworthy. But are the *means* (cheating) either wise or right? Doesn't common sense demand that *both* motive and means be right?

We know the answer to that one. But you see our advantage here. We come to humans with good motives, and tell them they can ignore the morality of means because "love makes it right." With humans who are legalists we stress moral means . . . and never let them evaluate the motives for their actions.

In either case we have a mixed good. We have a totally confused human, who does the wrong thing from the right motive, or the right thing from a wrong or inadequate motive.

Yes, "love" is wonderful—a wonderful tool for you and me. Using the word *love* to confuse, we can keep humans from the ways of Heaven, and they will never even realize they are living by the ethics of Hell.

LECTURE FOURTEEN

Thursday, 28 February 32913

Love: The Enemy's Way

Last lecture I spoke about *love* as we use that word to sow confusion. Today we have a most unpleasant task. We have to explore how the Enemy uses love. We have to examine the dynamics of Enemy ethics.

This is as uncomfortable for me as it is for you. We all much prefer the dank, dark, confusing maze of half-truth and untruth to the blinding simplicity and brightness of His pathway. Even thinking about Him causes us an inward shudder. To actually give His thoughts our whole attention is suffering indeed. But in spite of the pain we must look closely at love as the heart of the Enemy's way. So steel yourselves, grip the arms of your chairs. And bear it, if you will pardon the disgusting expression, "manfully."

I mentioned Tuesday that, to communicate His idea of love, the Enemy took a neutral Greek word, *agape,* and gave it strength and vitality. He gave it new meaning by using it to describe His own Invasion of our world, and His totally inexplicable surrender to Calvary. Before the Enemy came, "love" to humans essentially meant reciprocity. It was admitted that at times humans go beyond this to self-sacrificial love, but it was totally unknown for a human to show self-sacrificial love to a stranger or an enemy.

Yet the Enemy showed just this kind of love. As His book says, "very rarely will anyone die for a righteous man, though for a good man someone might possibly dare to die. But God demonstrates His own love for us in this: While we were still sinners, Christ died for us."

In the Enemy's system love does have dimensions of attraction and affection, and passion as well. To Him these are not wrong. But the element that transforms love into a vital ethical power is

His unique love, *agape*. That love chooses to spend itself freely for others, regardless of whether that love is returned.

If others fail to show the Enemy affection, He loves them anyway. If others are not attracted to His ways, He loves them anyway. If others actively reject Him, and prove themselves His enemies, He loves them anyway. He loved enough to give even His life for their sakes.

When the Enemy makes ethical statements such as, "he who loves his fellow man has fulfilled the law," He means the kind of love He showed mankind by His death.

Now let's recall another notion—that "love" is sufficient as well as necessary in ethics. This is the idea we promote when we imply that motive is everything, and means are ethically neutral or purified by the motive. In our ethical system a lie, told with the desire to help another, is promoted as a fully moral act.

But the Enemy says that one who loves will "fulfill the law." He explains it this way. "The commandments, 'Do not commit adultery,' 'Do not murder,' 'Do not steal,' 'Do not covet,' and whatever other commandments there may be, are summed up in this one rule: 'Love your neighbor as yourself.' Love does no harm to its neighbor. Therefore love is the fulfillment of the law."

Notice what the Enemy has done. He has removed conflict between motive and means by saying simply that *the means expressed by His Law are loving!* There is no conflict between wanting the best for others, and choosing to live by the Enemy's rules, because His rules show us how to truly love.

No one who really wants the best for another ever commits adultery. No one who seeks another's good steals. His commandments are designed by the Enemy to help humans love each other wisely and well. The Enemy's rules are not barriers to thwart humans who love and so desire to do good. The Enemy's rules are a highway down which true lovers walk.

It is *we* who have encouraged humans to think that love and law are opposites. It is we who have insisted that motive is all, and if a rule of the Enemy seems in a given situation to stand in the way of showing love, the rule must be broken. And humans have bought our fiction! These clods cannot even see that anyone who loves as deeply as God would never give rules that did anything but express love from beginning to end!

So far, then, in describing Enemy ethics I have simply said that 1) it involves motives which reflect His own self-giving love, and

2) it expresses that love in complete harmony with the Enemy's law.

But there is more to Enemy ethics than this. There is a supernatural dimension which can never be reduced to lists or rules, and cannot even be deduced by observing others' actions. Relationship with the Enemy is involved—a believer's secret relationship which we struggle to overhear, but even when listening hardest can catch only a distant murmuring within the human's heart.

What we know of that relationship we know only from things revealed in the Enemy's handbook. Only humans can know it by experience, and in that one thing they are far beyond us. Still, we can sum up the relationship in these statements:

* Love motivates obedience
* Love listens for the Enemy's voice
* Love values other persons supremely

Please control your stomachs as we examine each of these mysteries:

1. *Love motivates obedience.* Almost as great a wonder as Calvary is the love relationship that grows between the Enemy and one of His grubby "children." "Here is love," Calvary shouts to them, "not that we loved God, but that He loved us and sent His son as an atoning sacrifice for our sins." When they discover that love and faith quickens deadness into life, they are what He calls "born again." A great, surging vitality floods them as God's Word plants His own life deep within their personalities.

In spite of all our efforts, that life is so dynamic that it *will* grow. We can pour the cold concrete of our ethics all over their thinking, and that new life will struggle until cracks appear. Somehow the green freshness of His planting breaks through. Often we keep the plant from growing to full fruition. But we cannot destroy that life. We can stunt, but never entirely halt its growth.

The vital power that causes humans to grow is love. "If you love Me," the Invader said, "you will keep my commandments." This is not a threat, or words of condemnation; it is a simple statement of fact. Love for the Enemy, nurtured by worship and praise and feeding on His Word, is the key to obedience. Love is the secret of faith's power.

You see, love frees a human to trust. They are told to "walk by faith." And every step of obedience to God takes great faith, for no human can see ahead to the outcome of his choices. Faith always involves risk—stepping out into the unknown. Faith always involves an obedience that is based on trust rather than knowledge of outcomes. *It is at this point that the Person humans trust and obey becomes the critical issue.* If there is a deep love relationship between a human and God, the human is totally confident of his "Father's" commitment to care, and he is free to trust. If the human actually loves this "Father" of his, the human *wants* to obey . . . and will obey.

Our only hope is to introduce some other factor to warp the simplicity of that love relationship. We tell humans to obey because they "ought to." And soon they feel guilt instead of forgiveness when they fail. We tell humans to look to the stone god of law. And they struggle to obey rules rather than simply responding to the Father's words of loving invitation. Anything that distracts from the love of God and love for God drains the vitality of a Follower's relationship with Him. Any such things will contaminate a truly ethical life.

2. *Love listens for the Enemy's voice.* Most human ethical systems attempt to define what is "right." They set up hierarchies, examine principles, list priorities, and give rules.

The first thing to check, some will say, is whether there is a clear absolute (a "thou shalt not"). Second, you check whether there is an authority to which you are subject. Third, you examine . . . and so on. Why, some human ethics texts even develop hierarchies of priorities, and suggest a believer make decisions by working up or down the list until he finds "the" principle that applies and supersedes the others!

What these humans fortunately misunderstand is that their choices must always be made in the context of personal relationship. And that they are made with personal guidance from the Enemy Himself.

This is true of such ethically neutral choices as what college to go to, or what job to take, or what house to buy. It is also true of ethically potent choices.

For instance, one client of an acquaintance of mine was lost to the Enemy because a follower listened to God's voice, and not to the convictions of other Christians. This man, Bill, used to go into a local bar. He'd sit there evenings, drinking ginger ale. From time to time he would strike up conversations, adding in his quiet way a word for the Enemy. A young schoolteacher used to stop in the bar after classes each day for a glass of beer. He was quite arrogant, and not terribly nice. But after several months Bill struck up a conversation. In time the young man was won over to the Enemy, after a struggle during which, all unknown to him, Bill and three friends had prayed all night.

Now what's so interesting is that Bill was not welcome in the evangelical churches in that town. Why? Because he spent time in the town bar!

Would any of the other believers in that town have gone into the bar? Never! Their "rules" said that it was wrong. And they were listening for their rules, not for the voice of the Enemy. By their conventions the old evangelist was not acceptable. Yet it was he who listened to the Enemy's voice, and who snatched more than one human out of our clutches.

Ah, how wonderful it would be if all the Enemy's followers would just list their rules, and follow their principles, and set up their priorities . . . and never never stop to listen to the Enemy who does speak to them in a distinct voice. As the Invader said, "My sheep hear my voice, and they follow me." This is what God wants in all of humans' relationships with Him. This is certainly how ethical choices are to be made. God wants them to love Him and to listen to Him. If they listen, He *will* speak.

Humans who want a rational approach to ethics are troubled at the "mysticism" of this view. Good! Let them object. And let them studiously work out their alternate systems. (Though why they object to God having a contemporary voice is hard to grasp. Why, their theology insists that He is a living being who intervenes in the world of men. I suppose it's because for many of that type, their system is their god, and the Person with whom their relationship exists is relegated to second place. To *our* delight.)

How do humans hear God's voice? That is a mystery we cannot penetrate. We know the Enemy speaks through his handbook; we know that His Spirit focuses their attention on a truth or incident they've heard many times, and somehow they *know* that He is guiding them through the words. We know the Enemy speaks through other followers of His, with words of encouragement or counsel or rebuke. Amid often conflicting advice, a human will somehow hear and recognize one voice as His. We know the Enemy even speaks through circumstances. But how? That we cannot tell.

And we know one more thing. When humans do hear and follow His voice, they never break the Word He has spoken. The promise relayed to them by that troublemaker Paul is true: "all the righteousness of the law is met fully in us, who live not according to the sinful nature but according to the Spirit."

3. *Love values other persons supremely.* So far we have seen two dimensions of Enemy ethics. The first is that power to live an ethical life comes from a vital love relationship between child and Father. It is love alone that is powerful enough to free a human to trust and to obey. It is love alone that motivates obedience.

The second dimension of Enemy ethics is this. The Enemy Himself gives personal guidance to each child who listens for His voice. This is what Paul meant when he spoke of the Invader in these words: "Christ died and returned to life so that he might be the Lord of both the dead and the living." And Paul adds, "Why then do you judge or look down on your brother?" The Enemy claims the right to be sole and personal Lord in each follower's life. Each individual is to look to Him—not to human rules or conventions—for direction. When the human hears the voice of the Enemy, then he must follow.

Christians need to give each other freedom, and recognize that another individual's response to the voice may not be the same as their own. After all, the Enemy says again "the spiritual man makes judgments about all things, but he himself is not subject to any man's judgment." Such "spiritual men," who are led by God's Spirit, "have the mind of Christ."

Now, we want men to react to this teaching by screaming that it is "subjective." Particularly, let them worry that an individual might do something that *they* disapprove of (as if *they* were Lord!).

Be sure to point out to them all the immature believers who make honest mistakes and later are corrected from the Enemy's handbook. Give humans no time to consider that any growing child will make mistakes. Never let them realize that a wise father does not react by tying a child down with ropes to keep him from making another error. A wise father knows that the child will learn through his mistakes. So hurry these believers, and especially their clergy, to tie one another down tightly with strict rules and lists of dos and don'ts which "interpret" the Scriptures—and go beyond them.

I mentioned one objective criterion the Enemy's followers can use to test their hearing of His voice. His voice never contradicts

His Word. Actually, there is another. That criterion is: God loves persons supremely.

This criterion is good for them to use where there is no sharp "thou shalt not" or "thou shalt." When a choice is not guided by a biblical absolute (and few are!), then believers are to give others freedom to follow the voice of God. Yet each individual must test His own sensitivity to the voice. Is he hearing God speak, or is he hearing his fleshly desires? Is he hearing God, or the voices of fallible humans who rush to make rules for themselves and others?

Love gives guidance here by requiring that believers test all voices by the Enemy's known concern for all humans. Is the conviction "Christians never enter bars" the voice of God, or the voice of men? For Bill, the "sin by association" notion of the church community conflicted with a voice which said, "There are lost men and women in that bar I want you to find." When the notions of a Christian community become rules that cut a believer off from lost humans, then a voice that says "Go reach them for Me" is likely to be His.

It is to our great glory that most public opinion in the Enemy's churches echos our voice rather than His. He is not so petty, and has always been willing to set aside convention to show mercy or compassion, just as the Invader Himself did when He was on earth keeping company with publicans and sinners.

So this, in a very inadequate sketch, is what Enemy ethics is all about. It's about a love relationship with God that moves humans to respond obediently to His Word. It's about a personal relationship in which He, as Lord, guides each individually by His voice. It's about a growing relationship in which misunderstandings of the voice are corrected gently over time by the written Word and by a deepening awareness that the Enemy's supreme concern is human beings.

And that, class, is all *I* can stomach.

I have forced myself, for your instruction, to mouth words almost as if I were on His side, instead of committed to battle Him as Enemy to the end.

The one great consolation I have is this. The Enemy's way is a way that few of His followers really grasp. Many of them actually fear it. They long for the safety of a morality of rules and regulation. When the Enemy does not give them enough absolutes, they busily create a great host of their own. They sing of being "saved by grace," and proceed to deny grace in their attempt to live legalistically. In their futile search for certainty and security, they experience only momentary floods of that power for new life which He makes available.

We will not stamp out the new life. The greening vitality of it will break through any barriers we erect. We can stunt their growth, yes. But if they ever give themselves over to be swept up by His love, to listen passionately for His voice and to respond in raptured obedience . . . then they will know life in its fullness, and never, never be trapped in the web of our ethics of Hell.

 UNDERWORLD UNIVERSITY

February 29, 32913

Glubnose
Observer
Level 14

My dear Glubnose:

Imagine! My time is almost over here. Just four
more lectures. Why, I almost feel a twinge of
sorrow at the thought of leaving my classes. But
I do yearn to return to the battle. . . and to enjoy
to the full (while there is still time) the
pleasures of warping human lives.

At any rate, my reason for this letter is simple.
I forward with it a copy of the examination I gave
my students yesterday on the second part of this
ethics course. I wonder, Glubnose, if you dare try
to answer it? I know you've followed the lectures
closely, for you've been searching desperately
for some error to condemn. (Sorry, old ass, but
every lecture has clearly served the purposes of
Our Father Below, as even you with your dim wits
must have seen.) At any rate, do try. Take the
exam, and jot down your thoughts. If you dare,
send them back and let me grade them for you.

Why, I'll wager even a human reader of my words would
be able to do better on this test than you. Of
course, humans will never see my lectures in print,
much less my examination, thank Hell. In the
meantime, take my challenge.

If you dare.

Contemptuously,

Screwloose

Screwloose

Ethics of Hell
Professor Screwloose
Spring Quarter, 32913

Quiz Two

True/False: Fill in each blank with a T or an F.

_____ 1. Divine and human laws both are rooted in the Enemy's personality and character.

_____ 2. Divine law and human law have distinctly different functions.

_____ 3. Demons should always keep humans away from divine law.

_____ 4. Human beings who reject the Enemy have freedom to do as they choose.

_____ 5. The ethics of Heaven offers only a choice between slaveries.

_____ 6. "Authority" involves the claim by one person of the right to direct or control another.

_____ 7. There is an ethics of Hell both for those under authority and for those in authority.

_____ 8. "Truth" can be viewed as subjective or objective.

_____ 9. The contemporary idea of "truth" is comparable to the classical idea of "opinion."

_____ 10. There is no way to really tell whether a subjective moral "truth" helps or harms.

_____ 11. Truth in the Enemy's system means a statement of doctrine or fact which is in harmony with what He has revealed.

_____ 12. Guilt feelings are spoken of often in the Enemy's book.

_____ 13. Humans are moral beings.

_____ 14. Guilt involves recognizing and accepting responsibility for one's actions.

_____ 15. If a person feels guilty he will want to turn to the Enemy and look for forgiveness.

_____ 16. "Forgiveness" is likely to promote license if it is too freely offered.

_____ 17. The Enemy offers forgiveness to all who are sorry for their sins.

_____ 18. The phrase, "I love you," is ethically meaningless.

_____ 19. It is love alone that makes an act ethical.

_____ 20. Love in Enemy ethics fulfills His law.

PART III

The Opportunities of Ethics:
Contemporary Issues

LECTURE FIFTEEN
Tuesday, 4 March 32913

Capital Punishment: Societal Imperatives

What fun to watch a newscast these days. There are demonstrators screaming at each other over abortion and the "right to life." Others demand shutdown of nuclear plants. There are impassioned debates about the "crime" of capital punishment. Homosexuals sponsor liberation day parades which public officials attend to show support (and gain the votes of gays). Women complain about oppression and want to be called by the name of a magazine. There are committees to legalize marijuana, pornography trials, and loud debates about the "freedom of the press" to suppress evidence in criminal trials. And unindicted legislators admit to crimes at least as bad as those that forced a recent president to resign . . . and then are welcomed back by their fellows and reelected by their constituents.

Ah, class, this is a deliciously confusing time. It is a time of ethical dilemma . . . an opportune time for us. These issues, and many others, are doorways through which we can edge with our ethics of Hell. Each is a chance to confuse not only society but also individuals so that, whichever side of an issue one may be on, he will fight for his "just" cause in most unjust ways.

My last four lectures this term cannot touch on all the ethical opportunities that exist today. There are too many for that! What I wish to do instead is to take four issues, representative of broad categories in which other issues may be filed. I want to help you sort through some of the questions and, most of all, help you take advantage of the opportunities they give to distort your clients' lives.

First then, and quickly because our time is short, here are the four categories at which we'll look. One category is that of *societal imperative:* what responsibility is laid on governments to establish standards? Another category is *personal doctrine:* what issues of right and wrong does the Enemy leave to each individual to decide? A third area is one of *private depravity:* what admitted sins may be done in one's own dark, but no people may condone in the light? And finally, there is *cultural distortion:* what issues have grown within a culture till notions which are wrong have gained acceptance through common practice?

This chart, placed on the board, will tell you the focus of each lecture, and the particular contemporary issue I've chosen to illustrate the type.

1. Societal Imperative .... Capital Punishment	3. Cultural Distortion .... Women's Liberation
2. Private Depravity .... Homosexuality	4. Personal Doctrine .... Abortion

Now, let's move on. Today we view capital punishment as an illustration of an issue that involves a moral charge laid on governments.

Capital Punishment

It's instructive to listen in on debates between those for and those against capital punishment. Here are a few arguments I've overheard through a client's ears. Join me in your imagination as we reconstruct a debate:

Con. "Of course it's necessary that murders be punished, and with the ultimate punishment society can normally impose!"

Pro. "Ah, then you agree murderers should be executed!"

Con. "Never! That would make the government as bad as the killer. It would become a murderer too."

Pro. "You mean you don't see the difference between cold-blooded murder and judicial execution?"

Con. "The Bible says 'Thou shalt not kill.' All killing is wrong."

Pro. "Hey, wait a minute. That commandment is 'Thou shalt not murder.' Why, the Bible itself prescribes execution for murders."

Con. "That was Old Testament, when people thought of God as a God of vengeance. The New Testament portrays God as a God of forgiveness. The New Testament never prescribes capital punishment."

Pro. "So you'd let a person like Adolph Eichman, who took millions of Jewish lives under Hitler, go on living? Can't you conceive of murders so horrible that society's only possible response is to execute the killer?"

Con. "Why should we sink to the level of an Eichman? Of course he should be punished. With life in prison."

Pro. "Listen. That life-in-prison penalty never turns out to be life. It can be as short as six or seven years! What kind of deterrent is that to murder? We've got to make people think twice before they kill another human being. If they know they'll pay with their own lives for murder, there'll be a lot fewer murders."

Con. "Not true. Study after study has shown that the death penalty is no deterrent."

Pro. "What kind of studies? And who made them?"

Con. "Statistical studies comparing states with the death penalty on the books with those that have life sentences. Of course they were made by people like me, who are concerned that we set a humanitarian example."

Pro. "I've examined your studies. Every one of them has been criticized as irrelevant or faulty. Most studies were of states with the penalty 'on the books,' but not actually being assessed, while the Supreme Court has been overturning law after law. Besides which, polls show that the great majority of American people think the death penalty *is* a deterrent."

Con. "Let's get one thing straight. There is absolutely no evidence that the death penalty does deter. Without such evidence, we have no need to sink to the level of murderers by killing the killers."

Pro. "Well, execution at least deters the murderer from murdering again. More than one 'life sentence' killer has killed in prison, or escaped from prison to kill innocent people, or has been released after serving his time and then killed again. If the death penalty deterred even one person from killing another, it would have performed a valuable function."

Con. "But what about people convicted of a crime who are

later found to be innocent? If they're in prison, we can pardon them. But if we execute them, it's too late. I say if we save even one innocent life by removing the death penalty, we've performed that 'valuable function' you talk about.

"Besides, the death penalty in this country has always been administered unfairly. It's not murderers who are executed. It's *poor* murderers, from racial minorities, who can't afford good lawyers, who are executed. As long as the law is administered so unfairly we should call a halt to capital punishment. We must change social conditions, perhaps over several generations, before a death penalty law could be administered fairly."

Pro. "But that is exactly what the Supreme Court is forcing states to correct. Most laws on the books now protect against just such inequities."

Con. "Those changes in the laws may move in the right direction, but they aren't going to correct the problem. It's going to take generations before the impact of racial bias and sex bias is removed from our society. Until then it will be impossible for, say, a black who has murdered a white to get a fair trial in comparison with a white who has murdered a black."

Pro. "But how many times do murders take place across racial lines? Listen, the black community *wants* the protection provided by the death penalty, because the person a black is most likely to kill is another black, just as the person a white is most likely to kill is another white."

Con. "What we're talking about here is not who is most likely to kill whom. We're talking about basic inequities in administering capital punishment laws. The fact remains that, with our present system, some killers will walk away free or get light sentences while others will be executed—because of those inequities."

Pro. "You're saying that because the law isn't administered the same in each case, the death penalty should never be imposed?"

Con. "Yes, I am."

Pro. "Then by your reasoning anyone who is a minority or poor or can't afford a good lawyer should never be punished for any crime, because the law would necessarily be administered inequitably."

Con. "No, I'm saying that the death penalty shouldn't be imposed."

Pro. "So in the case of capital punishment we should use a different standard than we use to deal with other crimes and criminals? That makes no sense at all. Especially when the laws currently on the books in many states guard against inequities. Some even provide funds to hire the best lawyers for those accused of murder.

"You know, I get really fed up with all this coddling of the killer. No one ever thinks of the victim any more."

Con. "Of course there is concern for the victim! In fact, many of us who are against the death penalty are leading the fight for public funds to be made available for the victims of crimes and their families."

Pro. "I think we need compassion for the victims of crimes too. But I would much rather have capital punishment for murderers and see to it there were fewer victims in the first place."

Con. "Oh, come now. You're right back to that deterrent argument. We both know there is no proof that capital punishment is a deterrent."

Pro. "If the death penalty is a deterrent, some lives are going to be saved. Simply because there's no 'proof' that convinces you, why take the risk of removing capital punishment?

"And it just isn't *right* to let murderers get away with their crimes."

Con. "No one wants to let a murderer get away with a crime. What we're debating is the penalty that is *right* for society to demand. I say that the ultimate punishment ought to be life in prison."

Pro. "And I say the ultimate penalty ought to be death."

And I, class, say that we can enjoy all such exercises. Both sides have avoided the key question!

All humans agree more or less that the state, or government, or whatever they wish to call it, has responsibility for making and enforcing laws which promote the general welfare. What they disagree on are the limits to which this responsibility extends, and how "right" or "wrong" distinctions about laws are to be made.

For instance, motorcyclists are regularly bounced and battered by automobiles as they travel the streets and roads of the United States. Does a state have the right or obligation to demand that cyclists wear helmets? At times when such laws have been passed cyclists have mounted protests against such an invasion of their "rights." In some states, their pressure caused the state legislature to repeal a helmet law. The day of the repeal in one state, two cyclists smashed their heads in accidents and were killed.

Were the legislators at fault for surrendering a responsibility of government? Or were the cyclists simply exercising a rightful freedom foolishly?

Or take the case of pornography. Here freedom of the press suggests the right of publishers to print what they choose, and the right of individuals to select what they wish to muddy up their minds. But how far does this freedom extend? And who should have it? Adults over thirty? Teenagers? Should pornographic magazines be permitted that explore sex acts between "consenting adults" only? How about those that suggest group sex, or what moderns call "swinging"? What if the values promoted by a pornographic magazine are destructive of home and family, and thus threaten the stability of society? But go further. What if the pornographic materials in question exploit young children? At what point does government have the responsibility to say "stop!" and to insist, "This is wrong, and shall not be done"?

I've mentioned these additional cases not simply because we enjoy watching the frustrations of humans as they try to sort through complexities, nor just because we watch with glee as humans fill their thoughts with moral pollution that settles like soot to clog their choices and dirty their emotions. I've mentioned them because they represent some of the strange ways humans try to resolve the dilemma created by admitting that any government has the responsibility of making moral pronouncements and codifying them as laws which limit individual freedoms.

The motorcyclists insisted that a law requiring helmets was an infringement on their "rights" to go without . . . or, to put it another way, to kill or maim themselves without the interference of anyone. (Of course, the families will also demand the right to sue any motorist unfortunate enough to be involved in an accident where such a cyclist is bashed into idiocy.) The argument was accepted by the legislators.

But the same argument is not accepted when offered by those who want to legalize marijuana, or have unlimited access to pornography. Yet these are "individual" choices. Should governments interfere with an individual's freedom to do himself potential harm? (Each of these is a *possible* harm issue. Riding without a helmet does not make it *sure* a cyclist will be killed. Smoking marijuana does not guarantee that mind or motivation will be shaken. And most humans admit, even those most opposed, that poring over pornography may not make a person a sex fiend . . . if you'll pardon the absurd connection between us sexless fiends and that peculiar liability shared by humans and other animals.)

However sex, like capital punishment, is a much more emotional issue to most humans than helmets for cyclists. So a great outcry against permitting such materials to be sold has come from one group, while another group demands individual rights to wallow in filth if one wishes.

Now, how have humans attempted to resolve *that* issue? *By saying that pornography is wrong, but cannot be defined by the government:* "It's wrong . . . but we don't know what it is." Thus the courts finally determined that something is pornographic, and thus wrong, if it seriously offends the "standards of the community." What a fascinating notion! It is obviously based on contemporary relativism (the idea explored earlier that things are right or wrong "for me" but not for others). What the "community standards" concept does is extend relativism to majority vote, defining right or wrong as "for us," when "us" is the "community."

I suppose if a particular human community determined that the majority believed it right to kill all Jews (or all Palestinians), by that test such could be legally "right"!

Now, no human would really argue that way. Or not many. But notice where the confusion arises. It arises with the very basic question of how human governments are to determine what is right and what is wrong.

* Do individual rights override all other considerations?
* Do the feelings of a minority determine the standards of right and wrong?
* Are majority votes or polls to dominate?
* Is history (and thus traditional standards) to be the contemporary norm?

What then is the moral responsibility of governments? In the Enemy's scheme of things, which few take seriously these days, human governments are charged with making moral statements about righteousness and thus establishing and upholding His public standards.

Because humans are sinners, moral standards will always be different than moral practice. Adultery will not become right, even if a majority of people engage in it. But when a human society lowers its standards to match human behavior, unrighteousness is guaranteed.

Ultimately, although humans generally refuse to admit it, they must go outside themselves for standards of righteousness. Neither their behavior nor their ideas are truly accurate statements about right and wrong. Here the Enemy has, in His own disgusting way, provided guidance in His handbook. This is what makes debates on capital punishment rather amusing to us. Humans, even religious ones, argue diligently about what is "right," and then try to distinguish right and wrong by referring to their own moral sensibilities, or to what "most people" believe, or to whether or not capital punishment is a deterrent, or to whether there may be inequities in applying what laws there are, or to whether one innocent person might be executed by accident, or to whether one murder might be prevented by an execution, and so on. But if the believer wants to state the one argument which carries real weight, all he can say is that capital punishment makes God's kind of moral statement about the sanctity of human life.

Now, God does not speak out on all issues governed by human laws. He has nothing I know of to say about helmets for motorcyclists. I suspect that, since he says adultery is sin, He is not overly enthusiastic about pornography. But even humans ought to be aware that the Bible does speak out clearly on capital punishment. What does the Bible say? Well, the basic statement is in the Old Testament:

> From each man, too, I will demand an accounting for the life of his fellowman.
>> Whoever sheds the blood of man,
>>   by man shall his blood be shed;
>> for in the image of God
>>   has God made man.

To the Enemy, who values these beasts so, the crime of murder is such a terrible crime that no penalty other than death can express its horror.

Of course, the Enemy in His law made the same distinctions between accidental death and homicides committed in war or self-defense that humans make when they talk of "first degree" and other "degrees" of murder. In fact, I well recall how He established "cities of refuge" when he brought Israel into the

Promised Land, where a manslayer could flee and find safety unless he had done willful murder. But for willful murder, whether committed in the heat of passion or in cold blood, the Enemy prescribes death and that alone.

Nowhere does the Enemy suggest that this is prescribed as a matter of "deterrence." Instead, it is a matter of justice. And it establishes for all the true value of human life. Human life is so precious nothing but another life can be compared to it.

We've seen it often over the centuries. In a society where a life can be taken for all sorts of minor crimes, life is held cheaply. And in a society where life can never be taken judicially for any cause, life is also cheaply held. The one way to establish the sanctity of life, and to make that statement as a society, is to have only one crime for which life can be taken, and only one penalty for willful murder.

Of course, we demons care nothing for any of this. What we care about is our own satisfaction, and the erosion of human standards. Debate over capital punishment, ignoring as it does God's standards and struggling to find other criteria for "right" and "wrong," serves us well. So let them argue all the side issues. Let them debate inequity in administration of law. Let them affirm and deny deterrence. Let them insist on "community standards" for one set of laws and reject "community standards" for another. And let them argue with real heat, feeling a holy sense of righteous indignation no matter which side of the debate they are on.

As long as they never stop to ask on what basis governments are to judge their laws, and as long as they never look beyond their own moral sensibilities to seek a statement by God, we gain a profit. In the confusion that attends their debates, we will see the continued erosion of all standards and all laws . . . and soon individuals will feel quite free to reject whatever society may say. If at the last there is no external criterion of right and wrong to which men may look, then surely all becomes *opinion* and not *right*.

Every one of them, like you and me, will certainly prefer his own opinion over that of others . . . and over that of the God whom human laws and lawyers now ignore.

LECTURE SIXTEEN
Thursday, 6 March 32913

Homosexuality: Private Depravity

Liberation is quite the watchword these days. It began with women, but soon spread. There's a "theology of liberation" for South America. There's "children's lib" for those who think spankings or mean looks destroy youngsters' psyches. And, of course, there's "gay lib."

Each of these liberation movements campaigns for rights which people feel have been denied them. Some lib groups have a solid basis for their campaign in a distortion we've entrenched in human society. You know, as supposedly well-educated demons, that sin warps and twists society as well as individuals.

Some humans don't like this notion. They prefer to see sin simplistically, as an individual sort of thing only. Mostly it is "conservative" followers of the Enemy who want to battle sin one on one. "Just get an individual saved," they say, "and everything will be all right." They blithely ignore injustice and poverty and discrimination and all the other breeding grounds of our ethics.

Fortunately, such people are not close readers of the prophets, and so they fail to sense the stern anger of God against societal sins, and they fail to hear His demand that believers accept responsibility for the society in which they live as well as for personal righteousness. Usually such conservatives will view talk of any "liberation" with suspicion. They will automatically line up on the other side of the issue. Which means we have the glorious joke of suggesting to everyone that Christians are not only dull but also are in favor of "oppression."

These games with words are such fun for us to play. Our Department of Dissimulation has so confused the thinking of humans that to merely mention the word *liberation* these days conveys to most humans the highest moral and ethical tone, no matter what one is to be "liberated" from or for! Thus "gay liberation" (which insists society affirm their perversion as good rather than agree with God that it is evil) picks up many benefits from "women's liberation" (which asked men and institutions to face the fact that women have not been viewed nor treated as persons of equal value with men). In one case then, "liberation" demands sin be identified as good, and in the other case it demands that sin be identified as sin. Yet the same word is ascribed to both movements! And the humans, their puny mentalities confused, never make the distinction.

But now then, I have, as humans say, "let the cat out of the bag," haven't I? I've identified homosexuality as sin. In this we demons strangely find ourselves on the side of those followers of the Enemy who take His Word seriously. The difference is of course that we are *for* the sin of homosexuality, and any other sin, while they are *against* that sin and, supposedly, against all the other sins (except the ones they themselves indulge in).

But seriously, when we speak of this subject, we must be clear on the nature of this human practice. The Enemy surely is clear. In His Old Testament list of sexual practices that are not permitted is this statement about homosexuality: "Do not lie with a man as one lies with a woman; that is detestable." And the book continues, "everyone who does any of these detestable things— such persons must be cut off from the people. Keep my requirements and do not follow any of the detestable customs that were practiced before you came and do not defile yourselves with them, for I am the Lord your God."

Paul, in Romans, prates about futile thinking and darkened foolish hearts, and goes on about how departing from God led men to all sorts of sinful desires and practices. He calls "shameful lusts" and "impurity" and "degrading" such things as "men also abandoning natural relations with women and . . . inflamed with lust for one another." He continues, "Men committed indecent acts with other men, and received to themselves the due penalty for the perversion."

In view of such unmistakable condemnation of homosexual practices by the Enemy, it is a joy and delight to us to watch the confusion when homosexuals demand "liberation" and even approach churches (which, remember, are supposedly companies of followers of the Enemy and His ways) to be "married," to be admitted to membership *as homosexuals,* to be ordained as ministers, and in general to insist not simply that they be welcomed but that their practices be publicly declared acceptable.

As I say, what a laughable delight! The well-meaning follower, who believes in love and grace and forgiveness (and liberation) finds it hard to know how to deal with those who cry "liberation," and demand approval for their sin. The more conservative follower of the Enemy becomes so upset and uncomfortable at confrontation with this particular sin that he often attacks, or simply runs away to isolate himself from the practitioners.

Now as I said, it is all very fine if humans are confused by terms like *liberation* and, trapped by the general permissiveness of their age, hesitate to identify homosexuality as sin. But it is not helpful to us to be confused. We need to see clearly the nature of the perversion; partly so we can enjoy it more, and partly so we can hone our strategies to further confuse humans and keep them from dealing with the issues appropriately. Let's look at several areas we need to define for ourselves, and confuse for our human clients.

1. *Homosexuality and a secular society.* Human cultures throughout history have condemned, condoned, and ignored homosexuality. Unlike murder, which is clearly against the welfare of people in a state, and thus must be dealt with in any society, homosexuality is essentially a religious sin. One can empirically demonstrate that murder harms individuals, families, and even society. So all cultures have laws against murder, and establish penalties for breaking those laws. But it is arguable whether or not homosexuality is directly harmful in a societal sense. What it primarily harms is *individuals*.

Now God identifies all sorts of sexual sins beside homosexuality as harmful—adultery, incest, sodomy, promiscuity. These share with homosexuality His straightforward condemnation. But in general, as I said, such sins are not directly or immediately harmful *to society*. And so there is no particular basis, unless a state is theocratic, for specific laws against the homosexual.

Most sex sins distort interpersonal relationships and thus affect society, but do it so indirectly that the correspondence between action and result, unlike the case of murder or theft, cannot be immediately seen. The payoff, if we can use that term, is delayed. Society muddles on in a generally functional way whether its members are promiscuous in heterosexual or homosexual modes. Since there are no laws against general sexual activity between "consenting adults," there is really no basis in a secular society for establishing laws against the homosexual.

There are of course other ways beside laws by which societies define acceptable behavior and restrict members from unacceptable behavior. These ways express the conscience of a community, and involve kinds of social pressure, from half-joking remarks to outright attack or ostracism. Traditionally such forms of social pressure have restricted homosexuality and limited it to discreet, if not disguised, expression.

What is so interesting about the "gay liberation" movement in the United States (homosexuality is under quite rigid control in the rest of the Western world) is that liberation is not demanded from unjust *laws,* because there are no laws that discriminate against homosexuals as such. Communities may have laws against solicitation to homosexual acts. But homosexuals are not discriminated against by law for *being* homosexuals. There really is a significant difference. The latter would be laws such as "homosexuals cannot vote" or "homosexuals cannot hold public office." Since homosexuals do not need to be liberated from unjust laws, what then does the liberation movement demand?

The answer to that is simple. Gay liberation demands the banning of the forms of social pressure by which individuals express their conviction that homosexuality is *not* acceptable. Gay lib insists that society make official pronouncement that their private vice is both right and good. It cries for limits on the freedom of individuals (or school boards) to express "personal convictions" or the "standards of the community" in the choice of whom they hire.

This is one of the confusions that is hilarious to us. On what other issue can we demons be publicly on the side of sin . . . and win praise as being liberal and promoting freedom? How else can we disguise the rape of other human beings' freedom to express their convictions by calling for "liberation"? On what other issue can we demons encourage attacks on those who speak out against sin and, no matter what they might say or how they would protect homosexuals' legal rights, make them appear bigots and persecutors? What fun, young fiends, to twist evil to good, and good to evil, to the sound of cheering from those stupid cattle we intend to drag with us to eternal loss!

So here, then, is the distinction that we never want men to make. Even in a secular society, open homosexual acts may be legislated against, but homosexuals as persons should not be discriminated against by law. At the same time, the right of members of the community to express their own convictions for or against homosexuality should be maintained. Extending the right of private practice of any behavior hardly implies the right to impose acceptance of that behavior on others.

But don't be concerned. Humans hardly ever think this way. Before long, they'll be confused enough to believe it's wrong to have any moral convictions at all. And certainly wrong to give others the freedom to express convictions.

2. *Believers and homosexuality.* Since secular societies hardly pretend to be guided by the Enemy's thoughts, even true believers can hardly blame their government if it refuses to apply legal sanctions against homosexuality, to say nothing of hetero-sexual promiscuity, adultery, or any of the other private perversions that harm individuals without destroying society. Before long, I suspect, governments will even realize that prostitution, now identified by some as a "victimless crime," could be as great a source of revenue as gambling if properly supervised, and will legalize that oldest of professions.

However, there is a very basic difference between a secular society and one of the Enemy's communities. A church is not, in theory, a secular gathering. It is an assembly of those who have made a special commitment to the Enemy, and who have supposedly chosen to live in obedience to Him, or at least to attempt to live in obedience.

That's why it is so fascinating to see believers thrown into confusion. Homosexuals demand "church marriages," insist on membership when that involves acceptance of their private perversion as a "valid alternative lifestyle," and even ask for ordination to the ministry of the Enemy's "gospel," which proclaims freedom from the power of sin rather than the glories of bondage to it. And the majority of the Enemy's "disciples" hesitate to act as disciples and boldly state that their Master's words are binding! They don't boldly proclaim or prophetically announce to society that what the Lord God names as sin is sin. Nor do they insist that what He calls detestable, defiling, shameful, impure and degrading are in fact detestable, defiling, shameful, impure and degrading!

Some, of course, would never think of such a course because they view themselves as slightly more liberated than God. He might be bound by old-fashioned notions, but they, who know better than He the value of persons, would never criticize something so personal as a sexual preference!

That alone is rather amazing, as if sexual preference were the only issue. Anyone with any knowledge of homosexuality is aware that such a preference is developed usually by a series of homosexual *experiences.* Few people ever wake up one morning and say to themselves, "I think I'd rather marry a guy than a girl!" Almost no one moves chastely through a regular courtship process until he finds "the one," proposes, and then marries to form a lifetime union. Oh no! Homosexuality is *learned,* and usually through promiscuous sexual behavior.

If religious leaders won't criticize homosexuality as a perversion, why don't they at least criticize its promiscuity? Even heterosexual promiscuity before and after marriage is generally recognized by the Enemy's followers as sin. But no, these amazing Christians, who may believe that a one man/one woman union marked by faithfulness before and after marriage is right and good, not only hesitate to label homosexual activity as sin but never even challenge the promiscuity by which it is learned and with which most homosexuals live.

Amazing!

At any rate, do encourage confusion in the communities of the Enemy's followers. Let them cite God's love and compassion as reasons sin is not to be confronted. Let them improve on the Enemy's moral sensibilities, while ignoring or explaining away His clear statements. Never let them wonder why a promiscuous sex life which would never be condoned in heterosexuals is not even an issue in the discussion of homosexual "liberation" within the Church. And, of course, do stimulate homosexuals to insist on public acceptance of their perversion by the Churches. See to it they are never satisfied until they can publicly identify themselves, and still be welcomed as Sunday school teachers and as ministers of a God whose Word their lives deny.

3. *Believers' attitudes toward homosexuals.* Humans have such a terrible time separating sins and sinners. How laughable to see a follower of the Enemy meet a homosexual. He stands there frustrated, struggling with how to react. There are few less comfortable situations for a "straight." And the discomfort may be multiplied for believers, who after all have some responsibility to care for the individual, as little as they care for his or her perversion.

What is an appropriate response for Christians in individual meetings? What reactions do we want to make sure they avoid? Paul says in one of his miserable letters that the Enemy doesn't expect his followers to leave the world of human society and live in some isolated "holy" commune. He specifically says that believers are to associate freely with sexually immoral people in society . . . and are not even to judge them!

The Apostle's reasoning is simple. Believers should not *expect* unbelievers to live by God's standards. So believers are not to communicate condemnation, but instead to communicate love and hope. Christians usually fail to realize that the Enemy meets people where they are with His message of love. Believers fail to realize that a real and honest concern for any individual as a person is more important than implicit or explicit judgment of him for sins. Paul says, "What business is it of mine to judge those outside the church? God will judge those outside."

At this point we demons are dealing with really practical ethics. We are dealing with the daily choices individuals make in their real lives of here and now. As far as homosexual *practice* is concerned, Church and believer are to unhesitatingly identify it as the Enemy does and confess it to be sin. As far as the homosexual *person* is concerned, Church and believer are to ignore his perversion, and communicate the love and acceptance of God. The Enemy will handle judgment in due time. As for guilt, whether he admits it or not the homosexual already contends with guilt. A homosexual may be surprised at his sense of guilt, or angrily blame "society" for warping his conscience. But until the conscience is seared by much practice of sin, it will demonstrate guilt by accusing or excusing, just as the Enemy's book says.

So, in practice, homosexuality (no more than drunkenness, cursing, dishonesty, or any other sin a human may engage in) is not to become the focus of a disciple's attention in a relationship with another human. Instead followers of His are called to be gentle, long-suffering, kind, patient, loving, and all those other miserable "virtues" that the Enemy firmly believes will in some unknown way overcome the raw power of our vices.

That is the way the Enemy wants His followers to relate to those outside the community of faith. So we of course want to make a follower of the Enemy embarrassed, angry, or at least uncomfortable when he or she meets one of "them." On the other hand, we want to encourage the "liberation" movement among homosexuals, so that it will be nearly impossible for a homosexual to meet another human being simply as a person without insisting on being identified and accepted as a *homosexual* person. This obvious demand that acceptance carry approval is something few believers will handle well. So the push for liberation by homosexuals will effectively isolate them from believers who might have the grace to care about a person, but who will not betray their Master by extending approval to perversion as well.

One final thing. What about the homosexual in the Church? Well, if we can, let's whisper to believers that they must treat the brother who proclaims his vice and then demands acceptance in the same way they would treat an outsider—with acceptance and with love.

We must encourage this, for that course is a direct violation of the Enemy's way and His Word. In the same place Paul tells disciples not to judge outsiders, he says they are to "judge those inside." Indeed, he says that as a matter of discipline they "must not associate with anyone who calls himself a brother but is sexually immoral or greedy, an idolater or slanderer, a drunkard or swindler." A little later he says that "the wicked will not inherit the kingdom of God," and again points specifically to "the sexually immoral, idolater, adulterers, male prostitutes, homosexual offenders, thieves or greedy, drunkards or slanderers or swindlers."

All such things are to be rejected decisively by believers in their own practice. Because such activities are sin, and alienate a follower from fellowship with His Lord, they are also to alienate an offender from the Christian community. "Do not associate" is strong stuff, so strong that few among the Enemy's followers today even consider it. And that is fortunate for us. For a human who will not consider his sin to be a sin has no room in his life for repentance and forgiveness.

If the Enemy's churches did follow His words instead of human wisdom, they would find that isolation of sinners by the believing community is an act of love, for it forces the sinning follower to face his sin as sin, or to lose forever the fellowship of the family of God. Under discipline many have confessed their sin, and found in it restoration to health.

And this, of course, we do not want. We want depravities to rot the personalities of men and women. We love the putrid odors of every kind of sin, and so we spray on the perfume of words like *liberation*, hoping the sickness will spread unnoticed, even within the Enemy's camp.

And so hurrah for homosexuality! A sin that, though worse than other sexual sins, we promote to new respectability, and even introduce within the Church in such a way that those who take their stand with God seem greater sinners to most men than those who truly sin. Praise to the wisdom of Lucifer, my fiends. And ridicule to the foolishness of men.

LECTURE SEVENTEEN
Tuesday, 11 March 32913

Women's Lib: Cultural Distortions

It's been some time since Lord Chesterfield made a rather interesting series of observations about women. Listen as I quote him. You'll find these eighteenth-century notions quite instructive. Here are that nobleman's somewhat less than noble sentiments.

> Women are only children of larger growth; they have an entertaining rattle and sometimes wit; but not solid reasoning or good sense. . . .
> A man of sense only trifles with them, plays with them, humors and flatters them, as he does a slightly forward child. . . .
> Women are much more like each other than men; they have in truth but two passions, vanity and love; these are their universal characteristics.

Of course, men today would react with an outraged cry. Yet many women would simply nod their heads and say, "See?" To men, Chesterfield's raw chauvinism seems a thing of the past. But to many women his words reveal how they *still* feel—treated by men and society as large children, to be humored, but never seen as equals by men.

Today women are not treated as the equals of men. They don't receive equivalent pay for equal jobs. They are restricted by tradition to certain well-defined roles. They do not receive equal representation in such elective positions as city counsels, boards of supervisors, or Congress. And of course they are severely limited in all areas of life that approach the sacred. They aren't allowed to serve as priests or ministers. And no woman is allowed to take the umpire's high seat on center court at Wimbledon (which approaches the sacred in that land).

Now, it may be argued that traditionally women haven't been interested enough in nuclear engineering or election to Congress to bother with these unimportant toys which childish men enjoy. One might suggest that women have better insight into reality, and so prefer doing truly important things like being live-in mothers who shape the personalities of growing children and nurse the tender egos of the males who are the real "children of larger growth" of the human species.

Do try to get human males to make suggestions like this. They will infuriate the women even more. The females can then make remarks about "prefer being chained to the house and children!" and can shout a bit about the intellectual challenge of cleaning and washing and cooking and conversing with two-year-olds.

What we have here is a delightful situation in which nothing any man can ever say about the issue will please women. And in which no woman, even those who insist fulfillment is found in traditional roles, can help but feel at least slightly undervalued and put down.

When we involve followers of the Enemy in this wondrous debate, we really muddy the waters. Some say that "in Christ there is neither male nor female," quoting Paul's comment in one New Testament letter, and affirm equality. Others will loudly insist that since the "husband is the head of the wife," there exists a divine order of authority which shows the male is superior and the female inferior. This inferiority is rooted, they say, in the nature of women, and proves that the idea that females must keep their place in home and church is part of the divine pattern and not some male plot.

Please be sure, students, that discussions like these are conducted in such heat that humans never stop to explore their theological assumptions, or note how they have confused terms. They have made the biblical term *head* equivalent to "authoritarian control," while in the Enemy's system Christ as Head "gave Himself for" the Church. The Enemy's injunction to human males is no license to act the tyrant, but a command to follow the Invader's example and sacrifice to help develop the wife as a person. And by the way. No superior/inferior position implies personal inferiority. It only means that in a particular situation individuals have differing roles with differing obligations and responsibilities. Heavens! (if you'll pardon the curse.) Almost any worker knows deep down that he's far superior to that idiot who is his boss!

But it is a great thing for us that in human society tyranny of husbands over wives and superiority of men over women is generally thought to be the Enemy's position instead of ours, and His teaching rather than our lie.

All this is very entertaining for us. It is a good example of how perception of a class of persons can be developed over the centuries until real injustice results in a society. Humans systematically do discriminate—against women, against minorities, against the poor, and so on. Most individuals will argue that *they* don't discriminate. But the fact remains that today discrimination has deep roots in individual attitudes and in social structures.

This happy situation is only partly our doing. We seek to set group against group, color against color, status against status, religion against religion, and sex against sex. But humans are eager to do this themselves, without much prompting. The Enemy's law, as James writes in that book of his, insists followers show "no partiality as you hold the faith of our Lord Jesus Christ." But look at the makeup of any church board and see how many poor are on it . . . and wonder just a bit if only the successful in this world are spiritually mature. No, humans love to show partiality, and are always peering about for some group that they can act and feel superior to.

Happily, the Enemy's followers are likely to be insulted at charges of discrimination or chauvinism, and never examine their practices. The Enemy's followers are also unlikely to be disturbed at institutionalized discrimination. Few demand changes in society or church that might reflect at last the value the Enemy places on each human whatever the minor differences might be.

But enough of this general analysis. Our course is concerned with ethics. We are thinking about the impact of discrimination on individuals and how it can be used by us to promote hellish choices. So let's see how we can warp a truly "good" women's movement which seeks to restore a value stolen from them to our purposes.

1. *Encourage women to seek their identity in "accidents."* Ancient philosophy, which I'm ashamed to admit some acquaintance with, made distinction between "essence" and "accident." Essence has to do with the true nature of a thing. Accident describes a quality or property which can change without changing true nature. Once a school of philosophers, established in Athens some time after Plato, struggled to define the essence of "human being." Finally they came up with "hairless, featherless

biped." They were quite pleased with this definition until some wag tossed a plucked chicken over their wall. Needless to say, they went back to the definitional drawing board.

The Enemy's book does a better job of defining a human's essence. His definition is found on the earliest pages of Scripture, where it reports that God said, "Let us make man in our image." That *image* involves full participation in personhood. God is a Person, with emotion and intellect and will and every other capacity which, like creativity and appreciation of beauty, sets persons apart from the rest of animal creation. One can remove a human's arm, and he is still a being made in God's image. One can add extra fingers or toes, and the image is intact. One can add sin, and still a blurred image remains. One can also change a human's color, or dress one in finery or rags, or keep him in ignorance or give him an advanced education, and when you ask the critical question, "Is this a human being?" the answer always comes back, "Yes." The things men discriminate against in one another are always accidents and never essence.

How then about women? In the Creation story humans are told that God sent Adam on a quest for a companion. Adam explored the animal creation, but no one suitable could be found. Then the Enemy fashioned Eve from Adam's rib, and when the two met for the first time Adam knew her. "This at last is bone of my bones and flesh of my flesh!" They could be companions because, as Adam recognized, they shared the same identity! Both were human, shaped in the Enemy's image, and every aspect of personhood resonated and interacted in their relationship.

The sexual differences? Oh, very real. In some strange way we demons do not understand, it's even important. But the sexual difference is an *accident*. The essence of humanness is shared so men and women are to value themselves and one another equally as participants together in the crowning glory. They have been shaped by God to bear His image, and each has infinite worth and value to Him.

Now, it serves our purpose of confusion and distortion to influence both men and women so they see the accident of sex as essence. Get humans to define themselves as "men" or "women." Let them exaggerate the differences "we" have from "them."

This tactic has always worked effectively. When we get humans to exaggerate differences we develop hostility and reap all the benefits that come with suspicion, anger, and fear. We've done this historically with blacks and whites, with Protestants and

Catholics, with this tribe and that among Africans and Indians, with capital and labor. Why, with very little effort we've even stimulated glorious feuds between believers who hold the same doctrines over the kind of music to be used in Church, if any, and whether or not the waters of baptism should be sprinkled, poured, or used for dunking. In all such cases we soon have humans defining those who agree as "us," and those who differ as "them." Thus we encourage schism and division among His followers.

This is what we demons want most when it comes to an issue like women's liberation. Get humans to define each other by the accident of sex, and never, never let them address the issues that concern them from a solid base of essence. If each side would reason together, affirm one another as persons of worth and value to God and therefore to be listened to and treated with respect, the wrongs might be addressed fairly. Even if immediate changes in society could not be made, enough trust might develop so they could work together toward justice and love.

2. *Encourage women to feel that to be liberated they must be like men.* This is one of our really delicious perversions. In human society a number of behaviors and attributes have been associated with the masculine and feminine roles. According to these, men are supposed to be aggressive, competitive, and rational. Women are supposed to be supportive, cooperative, and emotional. Man's role in the "hunter" society, so the fiction goes, has historically been that of the provider, so all these "masculine" traits were required. On the other hand woman, as the pillar of the family, needed "feminine" virtues.

Some women, then, who have felt crushed by society or their father's disdain for girls have reacted. They demand equality, but see equality as a right to compete in the masculine arena. Thus many college girls now attach the same romantic reveries to careers they once attached to the white knight who would come and carry them away. Eager to compete, they have felt that to be equal with men they must be like men, and so have committed themselves to develop competitive, aggressive, and rational traits. It seems strange to us, but very helpful, that they never stop to wonder if these traditionally masculine traits are really *fine human qualities,* or expressions of sin. A quick look at the Enemy's handbook would enlighten them. For instance Christian leaders, the book says, are to be temperate, sensible, dignified, not drunkards, not violent but gentle, not quarrelsome (noncompetitive?), and not lovers of money. In another place it adds not arrogant nor quick-tempered, not greedy for gain but lovers of goodness, upright, holy, self-controlled.

Isn't it interesting that these qualities seem far more in harmony with traditional "feminine" qualities than with the "masculine" qualities associated with success? How delightful that we can encourage women to develop characters modeled on all that is ignoble in the "masculine" image, and to reject so many things that are truly noble because they are "feminine"!

There is one other strange twist that appears when we see this idea in the liberation camp. We find feminists who view liberation as competing with and becoming like men. Such women are as chauvinistic as the males they hate! In one place in the Enemy's book Paul talks about differences between men and women, and notes that there *are* differences . . . and that these were planned by the Enemy Himself. But the differences do not mean either is inferior or superior *in any way*. So many women who fail to glory in their femininity and try to become like men show that they have not accepted the Enemy's statement that they are worthwhile *as women*. They believe deep down they have to be like men to be significant.

If men fail to value women and do not treat them as equals, why then men are wrong and have wandered out of the Enemy's Way. But if women fail to value themselves or see themselves as equals *as women*, why then such women clearly are rejecting their value as much or more than are men.

So do encourage women to seek "liberation" by becoming more masculine. Be sure they choose only the most ignoble items from society's list of "masculine traits" to mimic. Then they will trot down our ethical pathway, even though they are in search of something which is in itself good.

3. *Inflame anger at limitations imposed by various roles.* No one ever supposed that humans live in a just society. All sorts of injustices exist, and all sorts of limitations are placed on individuals.

Now, followers of the Enemy should care about such injustices and work toward change. But change in institutions and society is made very slowly, usually over generations. From a human point of view this is too bad . . . and it's unacceptable to the impatient and the young. But it remains a fact that humans do live in an unjust world.

The question is, what can a human do to live an ethical life in spite of limitations? The Enemy's answer is simple: Live beautifully within them. It's not wrong to seek change. But when change does not come, then the follower must seize what opportunities he or she has to glorify God and to serve other humans.

We can shift the attention of many women from living an ethical personal life by making roles an issue. For instance, get women to feel they will never be truly liberated until one of them becomes President. Or get the religious to feel that they will never be liberated or able to serve the Enemy until ordained as priests or ministers. Get others to demand that women be recognized as elders or deacons. And make sure all feel rejected and unaccepted until such a role is theirs.

Whether or not these are valid roles for women is of no concern at all. Say that they are. Or say that they aren't. The issue is that women make possession of the *role* the *symbol of liberation.* If this becomes the driving focus in a woman's life, she will struggle for recognition and never realize that each follower of the Enemy in an unjust world must minister to others where he is. It is through ministry, not militancy, that gifts and calling are recognized. More important, from the Enemy's standpoint, fulfillment is found through ministering and caring and serving.

This brings us back to personhood, and to the one thing we never want humans to realize. Fulfillment as a person is never found in any accident. Fulfillment as a person is found in growing toward the Invader's likeness, and in reaching out to touch those around with God's love.

Whether a human has a particular role, or whether a role is unjustly denied, he or she *will* have opportunities to minister and to serve. It is on loving and serving that the Enemy wants His followers to concentrate. It is from these things that we want to distract them.

So let's distract all the women that we can by urging commitment to women's lib. Yes, it *is* a movement that seeks to correct a sinful fault in their society. But it is a movement against sin that we can encourage, for it has such potential to influence those who become involved.

A wise demon can use that crusade for our good and detour an individual into healthy sin. We can get humans to seek their identity in an accident, and destroy unity by labeling each other "them" and "we." We can get women to actually be ashamed of their sex, and to seek equality by developing all the most sinful traits associated with masculinity. And we can get women to so focus their energy on a demand for some symbolic role that they miss the opportunities in their present situations to serve with ministering love.

And so it is with all cultural distortions. As with the injury society has done women, we can put them to good use, and shape the ethics of Hell.

LECTURE EIGHTEEN
Thursday, 13 March 32913

Abortion: A Private Doctrine

In this final lecture, class, we look at the fourth type of contemporary ethical issue that provides us with opportunity to warp human lives and ethics. Let me review the other three so I can set this issue in contrast.

First, I spoke of opportunities relating to *societal imperatives*. In this area fall issues such as capital punishment, in which government must act because of the issue's direct and clear impact on society. There is no doubt that members of a society have to be protected against indiscriminate murder, for instance. So human governments must take a stand.

Second, I spoke of opportunities relating to some *private depravity*. In this category fall things which the Enemy calls sin, which social pressure in a community should discourage. However, with issues in this category there is no direct or clear threat to the society. So while a government may specify that certain acts are illegal when performed publicly or against another's will, in a secular society legislators will generally look the other way if the depravity is practiced discreetly by consenting adults. The fact that there may be no laws against a certain behavior does not make it moral. It simply means that, no matter how immoral, the behavior is not illegal. As you recall, I placed homosexuality in this category, along with a number of other sexual sins.

Third, I discussed opportunities which arise from some *cultural distortions*. Here all sorts of discrimination fit. In such things we work slowly over decades until attitudes of individuals, and institutions too, are warped and twisted by the sin of depersonalizing humans shaped in the image of God. I used women, in their current drive for liberation, as illustration.

Now in this fourth lecture I consider another kind of issue. I call these *issues of personal doctrine*. These are moral issues (and usually legal issues as well) in which there is enough uncertainty that humans cannot speak with *total confidence* that they know the mind of God for everyone.

Now immediately we hear objections from humans who are sure they know the mind of God in *everything*. This is something like the child who ran up to mommy with a teacup of sea water and announced, "Look, Mommy, I've got the ocean in my cup!" In each case the container is a trifle too small for what it is supposed to contain. However, as soon as the word *abortion* is mentioned there are *many* who are absolutely certain of the correct moral decision. The more emotionally significant any issue, the more certain those on each side will be that *we* are right and *they* are wrong.

This element of certainty is extremely helpful to us. When a human is sure that his position is absolutely right, he'll impute sinful motives to people who don't agree with him. In his certainty a human will never consider it possible that those on both sides could be trying honestly to work through a difficult issue as best they know how. So do encourage feelings of certainty. Stir up suspicion and anger. Use the wonderful legacy of fury that wells up in those crusading for the holy against the unholy.

However, before we get to the ethically practical aspects, let me give you some background on the abortion issue I've chosen to illustrate this type of opportunity.

Throughout human history, and across societies, humans have sought ways to avoid or void unwanted pregnancies. Moderns have more or less effective contraceptives. Ancients did not, although there were potions to stimulate miscarriage. But often a society, like that of the Greeks, simply used "exposure." This approach involved letting the mother go full term, and then examining the child produced. If it looked healthy and strong and was male, it would probably be kept. Otherwise, it was just tossed on a garbage heap to die. Likely four out of five girls born in Hellenistic times were exposed in this way. Quite often brothels were maintained by a proprietor who picked up abandoned baby girls and used them as household help until they were old enough to serve in an income-producing way.

Now, the Greeks saw nothing immoral about all this. After all, a baby was an *it*. It might *become* a true human being, but until officially recognized as such by the father, an infant was disposable and no great loss.

My point is simply this. As long as an infant was not considered to be a *person,* there was nothing illegal or to the Greek mind even immoral about disposing of it. However, once an infant reached a stage where it was recognized to be a person, *then* the infant had rights, and his or her treatment would be both moral and legal issues.

That background is important, because exactly the same issue is at stake in abortion. Humans who argue for abortion today speak about a mother's right to do what she chooses "with her own body." In referring to an abortion, they talk of removing "fetal tissue." This language carefully preserves the "freedom of choice" faction's distinction between what happens in an abortion and an injury that might be done to a living, independent person. On the other hand, the "right to life" group insists on speaking of an abortion as "killing an unborn child." They thus affirm that a developing fetus is a real human person, with moral and legal rights of his or her own.

In this kind of debate there is no room for compromise by either side. If the proabortionist admits that the fetus might possibly be considered a real human person, then abortion becomes murder. If the antiabortionist admits that the fetus might possibly be considered just tissue, then the right of the pregnant woman to do what she chooses with her own body can hardly be debated.

No matter what either side may shout, the real issue boils down to one thing and one thing only. When does an "it" become a real person? At conception? Three months along? Six months? On delivery? At one year of age? When the child can talk? Support itself? When?

In Western culture today there seems to be general agreement that by birth at least a child is a real human person. (Some cultures have put off naming, and thus personhood, for two or more years after birth!) But there is little agreement about when or if *before* birth a "human person" exists.

Antiabortionists insist that since the genetic code is stamped in a living cell at the fusion of sperm and egg, from that point the person who will be *is.* The living fetus will become the child just as a child will pass through many stages to become the adult. At all stages—fetus, infant, child, adolescent, whatever—the adult who will be exists in the imprint of chromosomes and genes.

Proabortionists argue vehemently against this. They say that perhaps a real human person exists when the mother feels movement within her womb. Or when the child can live as a separate being when removed from the safety of the womb. Each is convinced by his own arguments, and totally rejects the view of the opponents. Neither courts nor the medical profession dare make a "final pronouncement" on the issue.

Traditionally, it is the religious (and especially the Catholic) believer who has fought abortion, labeling it murder and insisting that the government pass laws against the crime. But the Enemy's documents are strangely silent. None of the apostles nor Jesus mentioned the still common practice of exposure. In the Old Testament, only oblique references can be found. For instance, one law requires that if a woman is struck and a miscarriage caused, the woman should be paid a redemption price. But the one causing the abortion is not tried for murder. And the price set is not as high as for a child or adult.

Still, to argue either way from the handbook's silence is hardly wise, though you can count on humans to do just this in support of their own side.

How then is an individual to decide whether she should have an abortion, or whether abortions are crimes that should be legislated against, or how to relate to a human who takes the opposite position? These dilemmas are glorious ethical opportunities for us—opportunities I want to show you how to take advantage of.

By the way. Don't ask me which side is *right*. I have my own idea, of course. But the mystery of how the Enemy works in creation of a new human personality is something none of us, much less humans, can say with authority. Anyway, it is ethically irrelevant to us which side is right. What is ethically relevant is that the conviction by each side that *it* is right gives us our opportunities. And here is how to use them.

Convince them they are absolutely right. The conviction "I'm right" and "They're wrong" is a wonderful thing. The more a person is convinced he's right, the more frustrated he will be when those pig-headed others don't see it his way. When the difference is over a significant moral and legal issue, then hot indignation will come and justify even fits of anger. Every human conflict can be intensified by a conviction of righteousness. There's nothing quite like the belief that "God is on our side" ("and the devil on theirs") to bring about inquisitions, wars, and other entertaining forms of persecution.

Such warfare is particularly vicious between believers. In their churches they will be particularly eager to crush opposition, and will certainly ostracize other believers who differ. Cutting things will be said. Hurts will be passed back and forth freely. And we will enjoy every scar.

There is only one way for humans to avoid the many ethical benefits that come to us from this kind of debate. That way is to adopt a most uncharacteristic humility. To admit that a bare possibility exists that "they" might (just might, mind you) be right and "we" wrong. It's very hard for humans to admit this possibility. It's especially hard when the issue is vital morally and legally. Of course, to admit the possibility does not mean anyone should hesitate to continue his efforts to influence courts or legislatures. All it means is that the certainty, which forces a human to question another's motives, must be abandoned if the human is to deal with the question in love.

Actually, the Enemy's book warns humans that "knowledge puffs up." It goes on to remind them that their knowledge is at best partial and imperfect. Instead of relating to others who differ from a position of superior knowledge, Paul reminds that "love builds up." He points out that when humans show love to others, they remove barriers and bring a possibility of mutual understanding and potential agreement.

Now whether humans ever agree on an issue like abortion is certainly of indifference to us. What we want out of their debate is that as many barriers as possible be erected between humans. We want humans to hide behind their walls and shoot their darts at each other. And we particularly enjoy it when followers of the Enemy shout angrily at the unconverted and link their particular position on abortion so closely with faith in the Enemy that the Invader is no longer the object of faith—the implication is that Christ *and* anti- or proabortion makes a person a Christian.

As I say, as long as humans are unwilling to approach an issue with some humility and admit their fallibility, we gain all these benefits with hardly any effort at all.

Insist they are responsible for everyone else. Many humans resist taking responsibility for their own actions, but still rush around insisting everyone else live by their convictions. This is a deceptive, and therefore a wonderful, thing for us. It's one thing to say, "I believe abortion (or remarriage, or some such thing) is wrong, and as a responsible moral agent will not do it." It's another thing to say, "I believe abortion is wrong, and I will not let you make your own responsible decision, but insist you act on my conscience."

Yet in many truly important areas, humans are left without enough guidance in the Enemy's handbook to say *positively* that a certain action is immoral. Even if they have enough evidence to be quite sure something is immoral (as is homosexuality), they still may not have a right to say that the thing *also* should be illegal! In such difficult cases humans should accept personal responsibility for their own choices, and extend to others the right of personal responsibility for their choices.

This is a very hard thing for humans to do. It's unlikely that many will. They seldom remember that the Invader died and rose that He might be Lord to each of them. Ultimately every human is responsible, not to another human, but to the Enemy Himself. But we'll certainly not remind them of *that!*

Instead we delight when humans arrogate God's prerogatives to themselves. We laugh when they insist that they, with their greater moral insight, are to lord it over others. Even when they are right about the issue, being right and being Lord do not go hand in hand.

Insist they judge others harshly. Humans seldom will be able to force their views on others. They'll try hard enough. But it's unlikely many will succeed. What then is left? Well, we can encourage humans to condemn each other enthusiastically.

Of course the Enemy tells His followers, "Who are you to pass judgment on the servant of another?" In another place He says, "He that speaks evil against a brother or judges a brother, speaks evil against the law and judges the law. But if you judge the law, you are not a doer of the law but a judge. There is one lawgiver and judge, he who is able to save and to destroy. But who are you that you judge your neighbor?" If humans followed His Word they would evaluate their attitude toward the others with whom they differ.

But they won't. And we will keep on whispering to them about how terrible it is to oppress a woman, or to kill the unborn. In the heat generated, humans generally can be counted on to lose all restraint, and even the Enemy's followers will act more like worldly men than the worldly do.

So what are our strategies and devices to distort the divine ethics through issues like abortion? We encourage humans to feel more and more positive that they are right, and the others wrong. We help humans feel sort of a divine calling to force their moral judgments on others. And if it happens that they are not in a position to impose their consciences, we at least make sure they judge one another harshly. Thus by word and deed and attitude they deny the spirit of the ethics of Heaven.

But now our class is almost over. I have one last announcement, and then you are dismissed. As a final exam, I am presenting you with a list of contemporary ethical issues. Your task is simply to classify them by the four categories we have explored together. Don't expect an answer key for this exercise. There will be so many disagreements that even a demon wouldn't dare to take a position.

And so, fiends, farewell. And do enjoy the misery you will bring to the human race.

While you still have time.

 UNDERWORLD UNIVERSITY

March 14, 32913

Kregsgelt.
Under Secretary,
Department of Education
Hell Central

Dear Kregsgelt,

I confess that when I was ordered to the post of visiting lecturer here I was angry. "What a waste of
time!" I felt. But in my time here I have had a
change of heart. I see the wisdom of your plan to
expose demons in training to field agents, and to
introduce a bit of the practical in the classroom.

I find I have actually enjoyed putting together in a
systematic form explanation of some of the devices
by which we lure humans further along the pathway
to hell chosen by the first pair. I have also found
the students here to be more alert young fiends than
I had expected, and I actually think several might
have learned significantly enough to become effective deceivers and tempters!

At any rate, I did think you ought to know that as
little as I like admitting a mistake, my first critical reaction was wrong. So please accept my congratulations for conceiving of this new dimension in demon
training, and my thanks for the opportunity to con-
tribute.

Sincerely,

Screwloose

P.S. I am even thinking of another series of lec-
tures--perhaps something along the lines of how to
spoil a believer's daily experience of the "normal
Christian life." If there's enough interest there
at Hell Central, it may be that Screwloose will lecture again!

Ethics of Hell
Professor Screwloose
Spring Quarter, 32912

Final Exam

Place each of the following contemporary ethical issues in one of the four categories below:

pornography	freedom of press
abortion	homosexuality
marijuana	gossip
hard drugs	remarriage
helmets for cyclists	child abuse
illegal aliens	smoking
suicide	Laetrile
55 mph speed limit	euthanasia
"right to work"	cloning
alcohol	sadism
pacifism	premarital cohabitation
divorce	rape
wife-beating	

Societal Imperative	Private Depravity	Cultural Distortion	Personal Doctrine

APPENDIX A

Quiz 1, p. 63

TRUE—FALSE

1. True. Uncomfortable sins might lead to conviction.

2. Plato to the contrary, this is patently false. Humans who know what is "good" will not necessarily do it in theory, and not very often in practice.

3. False. The Enemy is concerned with love-motivated obedience. *Intentions* are by definition *not yet* obedience.

4. False. As I pointed out in my lectures, emotions are themselves ethically neutral. "Sin" relates to human choices and actions, not to their feelings.

5. No. "Natural" is neither good nor evil.

6. Again, false. "Belief" refers to concepts or ideas. Many things that humans *believe* have no effect on their behavior.

7. False. Many humans will be so proud of believing the right things they will never even consider a need to act on their beliefs.

8. All too true.

9. Theologians differ on this one. What we demons discover is that if a human does respond, the Enemy enables him. Let the theologians argue about who initiates such actions. Let's keep the beasts from saying "I will" and doing it.

10. Not necessarily. The Bible is only dangerous to us or helpful to humans if they act on it. Getting them to study it "to find out" things is irrelevant to ethics—ours or His.

ESSAY

1. Strategies demons use with human emotions (see lecture 3):
    - We make emotions seem to be the ultimate reality.
    - We convince humans to "express" emotions by attacking others.
    - We tell humans that others are responsible for their feelings and keep them from accepting personal responsibility.

2. Strategies demons use with human beliefs (see lecture 5):
    - We insist humans focus on the truth or falsehood of their beliefs.
    - We stress the responsibility to believe correctly, to the extent that *practice* is ignored as unimportant.
    - We encourage pride in correct belief, which results in doctrinal divisions in God's family.

3. Strategies we demons use with motivations (see lecture 4):
    - We suggest that if a desire is "natural" it must be all right. After all, didn't God design human nature?
    - We warn that repressing passions is unhealthy.

4. Strategies we use with human wills (see lecture 6):
    - We confuse *intention* with action, so they feel good about what they *plan to do* . . . without doing it.
    - We convince them they cannot act significantly yet (until their situation changes, they grow older, get money, etc.).
    - We help them keep decisions so general that no specific action is taken.

5. Human emotions are "real" in the sense of being subjectively present. But feelings may not fit the reality of a situation. And feelings can change. Thus they are not a solid foundation for a human's life—something we never want the "feeling" person to realize.

6. A human who sees himself as weak will feel helpless when faced with a significant choice. Keep him focusing on himself and his inabilities, and he will *never* act in obedience.

7. Ethics is not related to good or bad motives in that "ethics" exists only in the realm of choice and action. Until motives are translated into action, they are quite irrelevant as "good" or "bad" aspects of a human's personality.

8. True beliefs can be turned to our advantage when we make agreement of belief a test of fellowship, rather than membership in

the Enemy's family. Also, belief can lead to pride, and pride in true belief can lead a believer to condemn or look down on a brother the Enemy wants him to love.

9. The ethics of Heaven calls on believers to hear God's voice and respond with obedience now. *We* want humans to think about what they *will do* someday, and thus put off today's obedience.

10. This you must answer for yourself!

Quiz 2, p. 125

TRUE—FALSE

1. False. Divine law is an expression of the character and personality of God. Human laws are traditions drawn from customs and rules of behavior which grew up over many years.

2. True. Human law is designed to give security and stability to society. Divine law has a different function: it reveals God and convicts humans that they stand guilty before the heavenly Judge.

3. False. Divine law can be very useful to demons, as long as its true function is hidden from humans. Some humans will see law as a challenge and try desperately to do it, ever commending themselves they are doing an acceptable job. This is a delight to demons who want humans to try harder, and never to admit defeat (and thus a need for forgiveness).

4. False. "Freedom" is a fantasy, in that humans are always limited by their natures and their circumstances. Morally they are "free" to choose to do wrong, but never free to do wrong safely or even comfortably.

5. True. The Enemy is very blunt on this. Humans can follow Him closely and become "slaves to righteousness" or can choose other ways to live and become "slaves to sin."

6. True, in general. Though the Enemy's authority is not authoritarian.

7. Very true! We want humans with authority to take it as a license from the Enemy to oppress, and those under authority to view it as a reason to rebel.

8. True. It *can* be viewed either way. Of course, it cannot *be* both. But that is not the question I asked. (Demonic, hey?)

9. True. When humans say something is "true for me," they are admitting that they are simply speaking of opinions. Everyone knows this. But of course, since *opinion* has no positive moral connotation, we want humans to use *true* in their own subjective, wishy-washy way.

10. True again. In morality and ethics there is usually a a long gap of time between actions and their moral outcome. Humans are left trying to make their "true for me" decisions on physical sensation alone—a very foolish thing.

11. Not really. Truth to the Enemy involves revelation of reality as He alone can know it. But truth to Him is to be experienced by His people, not simply verbalized in doctrinal statements.

12. Solidly false. He speaks of real guilt, not of guilt feelings. He doesn't even speak much about real guilt. Disgustingly, He seems to want to speak instead of forgiveness.

13. True. We see this not in that they *act* morally, but in that in spite of themselves they believe in right and wrong.

14. True as far as the Enemy is concerned. As for us, we want humans to *feel* guilty and yet deny their responsibility.

15. False, provided we're on the job. An alert demon will use guilt in his client's life to make the human run *from* the Enemy, not to Him.

16. False. We would *like* to believe this. Surely we want humans to believe it. But somehow our cursed Enemy offers the freest forgiveness of all . . . and in the process leads humans into holiness. It just doesn't seem fair!

17. Ah. Not true. There's an important point here. That "the Enemy offers forgiveness to all" is true enough. ". . . who are sorry" isn't, though we would like humans to think they "do something" to merit forgiveness. We'd like to add *anything* to that offer of forgiveness, to keep humans from realizing that it is the Invader's act, not theirs, that wins man forgiveness.

18. True, until it is explained what kind of love is meant. Of course, the word *love* (no matter what is really meant) is ethically positive. So we can use it, and urge humans to use it, to cover even the deepest selfishness.

19. Well, true . . . and false. Love is the *necessary motivation* for all acts stimulated by the ethics of Heaven. But love is not *sufficient*, for love requires direction to choose actions which are truly beneficial to others.

20. Disgustingly true. Love fulfills law, because His love seeks always what is best for others, and love, as an expression of God's goodness, shows the means by which humans can best do others good.

APPENDIX B
Scripture Index

While Screwloose usually did not give references in his lectures, he apparently alluded to the following passages at different points. Often Screwloose paraphrased; at other times, as for extended quotes, he seems to have used the New International Version of the Bible (NIV).

Lecture 1
p. 18—Gen. 1:26, 27, Heb. 2:7

Lecture 2
p. 30—John 15:5

Lecture 3
pp. 39–40—Col. 1:11 (much like J.B. Phillips's paraphrase)

Lecture 4
p. 46—2 Pet. 2:12; Jude 10

Lecture 5
p. 52—James 2:19
p. 53—2 Pet. 3:11
p. 56—Rom. 12:2

Lecture 6
p. 58—Heb. 3:7

Lecture 7
p. 73—Rom. 14:5–6
p. 74—Rom. 3:19, 20
p. 76—Rom. 8:4

Lecture 8
p. 79—Rom. 6:15–16
p. 80—Gal. 5:13

Lecture 9
p. 88—Heb. 13:17
p. 89—Matt. 20:25–27, NIV

Lecture 10
p. 93—Phil. 4:8–9
p. 95–96—John 8:31, 32

Lecture 11
p. 97—Rom. 2:14–15
p. 98—Rom. 3:10
p. 99—Rom. 2:15

Lecture 13
p. 113—Matt. 5:46–47

Lecture 14
p. 115—Rom. 5:6–7
p. 116—Rom. 13:8–9; Rom. 13:10
p. 117—John 14:15
p. 120—Rom. 8:4; 1 Cor. 2:15–16

Lecture 15
p. 136—Gen. 9:6, NIV

Lecture 16
p. 139—Lev. 18:23–25; Rom. 1:26–27
p. 144—1 Cor. 5:12
p. 145—1 Cor. 5:11; 6:9–10

Lecture 18
p. 158—1 Cor. 8:1–2
p. 159—Rom. 14:4; James 4:11–12